w. b. yeats
the later poetry

thomas parkinson

W.B.yeats
the later
poetry

Berkeley and Los Angeles

university of california press · 1964

UNIVERSITY OF CALIFORNIA PRESS
BERKELEY AND LOS ANGELES
CALIFORNIA

CAMBRIDGE UNIVERSITY PRESS
LONDON, ENGLAND

LIBRARY OF CONGRESS CATALOG CARD NUMBER: 64-13473

For Ariel, and the children

pReface

~.~.~.~.~.~.~.~.~.~.~.~.~.~.~.~.~.~.~

IN MY FIRST BOOK *on Yeats*
(W. B. Yeats, Self-Critic) *I examined the development
of Yeats from juvenilia to his mature period, and in this
book I consider the composition of the later poems,
both the process of shaping and the finished construction of the artifact. I am concerned with the principles
that motivated his writing, what he thought about poetry not only in general terms but in the detailed discriminations that he made in forming lines, qualifying
imagery, distancing experience. Hence the book moves
from principle to practice and back to principle, constantly checking general concept against particular*

choices and rejections. The manuscripts in the hands of his widow, Mrs. W. B. Yeats, represent the most comprehensive record of the processes of poetic composition that I know, and from them, along with the finished poems and Yeats's prose writings, I have tried to establish Yeats's poetics. The chapter divisions accord with the basic elements of Yeats's poetry, the first two chapters treating primarily his lyric dramaturgy, the third his use of symbol and image, the fourth his sense of measure (prosody).

In the opening chapter I treat first Yeats's attitude toward modern art in general and the concept of personality entertained by Eliot and Pound in particular. Yeats, largely because his life spanned both the late nineteenth and early twentieth centuries, participated in a wide range of attitudes toward the role of the person in poetry, and from this experience he formulated a lyric dramaturgy that is extremely inclusive and tough, an extension and critique of the dominant modern aesthetic. In considering his ideas I make extensive use of his Autobiography *but also test the ideas extrapolated from his expository prose by analyzing his poetic composition. This analysis is further extended in the second chapter, which also foreshadows the detailed considerations of the succeeding chapters.*

The third chapter, after an introductory analysis of the chief critical modes used in studies of Yeats's "symbolism," examines in detail the swan and the sun and moon as examples of Yeats's iconographic practice. I use the term "iconography," which is becoming the normal term in the vocabulary of Yeats's critics, because it has a wider connotation than either symbol or image and can be used to include both. The main point of the chapter is that his iconographic use is conditioned and qualified by the dramatic motives of the poems so that any given icon, even those that have supernatural weight, may have varying reference and prestige from poem to poem. Yeats moves with ease and rapidity from allegory to simple image, with a large body of possible reference between those inert extremes. The chapter concludes with an examination of the outcome, in Last Poems, *of his practice.*

The fourth chapter treats primarily Yeats's sense of linear measure, his prosodic idiom. The main modes of his prosody are either the stress line or the syllabic line; there is little reason for thinking that he wrote with a conscious sense of the foot. Since his prosodic choices were so affected by syntax, iconography, and dramaturgy, the necessarily detailed analyses of this chapter serve to resume the concepts developed in earlier chapters. The concluding chapter summarizes the main arguments of the book and suggests the relevance of Yeats's poetics to current poetic problems.

The main thesis of the book is that Yeats's poetry was largely determined by his dramatic sense. He thought of himself, even when composing lyric poetry, as answering to what he took to be the dramatic design of the universe. Attacking the problem of composition, he held in mind a wide range of poetic possibilities, dramatic, iconographic, and prosodic, and the complexity of his verse originates in his refusal to accept a mechanically simple set of solutions to any given poetic problem. His poems tend to grow away from their initial propositions, altering their motive as the opportunities for extension or complication appeared in the prosodic or iconographic pattern, and changing too as the spokesman's role in the poem became clear. The dramatic element in the poem had a determining effect on tone and structure, and, as he came in his later years to accept more readily the roles suggested or even imposed by his experience, his sensibility was liberated. His recklessness of external judgment compelled his verse to depths and reaches that had not hitherto been possible, and so the poetic texture had to expand and deepen. He profited also from his long development that granted him a wide range of experience with different poetic modes, and he renovated traditional forms and subjects in accord with his own deeply original sense of experience.

The result was a poetics, embodied poetically rather than thought out in discursive prose, but still rational and inclusive. This poetics is a critique and elaboration of major concepts in modern poetic theory, and its corrective force seems to me potentially very great. I try to suggest its importance in the conclusion to the book, but its relevance to current poetic problems is implicit throughout the text.

My debt to other students of Yeats is indicated in the footnotes, but I do wish to acknowledge my debt to the basic bibliographical work of Allan Wade and the variorum edition of G. D. P. Allt and Russell Alspach. During the several years in which I worked on this book, I had the opportunity to study the manuscripts of Yeats's later poems, first in Dublin and—thanks to the generosity of Mrs. W. B. Yeats—in reproduction in London and in Berkeley. To Mrs. Yeats I have the same debt that all students of Yeats feel toward that wise, witty, perceptive, and hospitable woman. Because of her generosity, and that of John and Madeleine Montague, my stay in Dublin was a delight. The National Library of Ireland was unfailingly coöperative, as was the British Museum. My extensive travel was undertaken during the tenure of a Guggenheim Fellowship, an honor and aid for which I am deeply grateful. The American Philosophical Society provided a travel grant, and the Committee on Research of the University of California was generous as always.

Many of my students have contributed to the shaping of the book, and two of them—Russell McGrath and Robert Mooney—typed large portions of the text and checked references with accuracy and good cheer. My colleagues George Elliott, Willard Farnham, Thomas Flanagan, Josephine Miles, and Mark Schorer read various versions of the text and made important suggestions. My sister Catherine typed a large section of the manuscript, and my wife Ariel gave me the Redon lithograph that is reproduced on the dust jacket and encouraged me by advice and example. The book is dedicated to her.

Parts of chapters i, ii, and iii have appeared in quite different form in The Journal of Aesthetics and Art Criticism, Modern Philology, *and the* Sewanee Review, *and I am grateful to their editors for permission to reprint them here. Grateful acknowledgment is tendered to The Macmillan Company, publishers of Yeats's poetry, for their long patience in corresponding on the subject, and for permission to quote so widely from works to which they hold the copyright:*

contents

the embodiment of truth

A man can embody truth but he cannot know it.

Study and Expression

WHEN the relation of poet to poem comes under discussion, the implied issue is, "What kind of knowledge is presented in a poem?" Is the poem itself a knowable object? Does it present knowledge of reality external to itself by a symbolic system of reference? Or does it present primarily knowledge of the writer, an exhibit of personality? And if it presents primarily subjective knowledge, why should we attend?

This issue has been aggravated in the period since the French Revolution by the increasing individualism of thought and the acceleration of breakdown in social purpose. In Henry Adams's language, the standard solutions have failed and each man has been forced to find

1

his own. The great writers of that era—our era—have been plagued by the problem of their own egotism, their necessity for thinking of their personality as privileged, their experience as at once unique and symbolic. They are self-assertive—Goethe, Wordsworth, Blake, Baudelaire, Whitman, Hugo, Rimbaud, Lawrence— and this self-assertion is compelled and distinguished by a personal point of view, an attitude deliberately formed and chosen that often hardens into a systematized philosophy. The great Romantic writer is not admired as embellisher of received ideas but as prophetic inventor.

The strain thus placed on a poet is considerable—the isolation, the temptation toward self-indulgence, toward superficial eccentricity of dress and manner as well as compulsive idiosyncracy of idea and style. Even the poet who chooses a conservative or archaic posture and a deliberately conventional manner can be driven to shrill hysteria. Thus, in spite of the protective devices of traditional style and ultraconservative ideas, a poet like Baudelaire found the stresses of the Romantic artist's life intolerable. His biography is one long running sore of resentment, betrayal, illness, and hatred. All he had was his integrity, his established—by such suffering— point of view. In the last years of his life he wrote to his antagonist, shadow, and protector Ancelle a description of the motives guiding *Les Fleurs du Mal:*

Must I say to you, who haven't guessed the truth any more than anyone else, that in that terrible book I've put my whole heart, my most tender feelings, all my religion—in a disguised form— and all my hatred? Even were I to write the contrary, and swear by all the gods, that it was only a composition of pure art, of artistic jugglery with words, a work of imitation—I know not what else—I'ld only be lying like a trooper.[1]

These sentences, torn from him by exasperation and despair (how could Ancelle have understood, ever?), have the tone of ultimate sincerity. It seems almost irreverent to take them coldly as typical of a general problem, and yet they do phrase compellingly the problem of poetic knowledge. For it is merely common sense that the act of articulating is a form of expression, that composition is self-revelation, that art however pure comes from the special, limited "rag-and-bone shop of the heart." And yet the poet is, at the same time, conceivable as detached maker, creator, imitator, even juggler.

Baudelaire's needs as man and poet were deeply confessional, and the disciplined expression of the heart's entire depth was the obsession of his work. The validation of that obsession lay in the representative range of the heart; we attend to him because he speaks what we dare not confess. But Yeats was only intermittently confessional in motive and being personally understood was not a primary desire underlying his work. When he considered, at the end of *his* life, the poet's expressive necessities, he was exultant:

I know for certain that my time will not be long. I have put away everything that can be put away that I may speak what I have to speak, and I find "expression" is a part of "study." In two or three weeks—I am now idle that I may rest after writing much verse—I will begin to write my most fundamental thought and the arrangement of thought which I am convinced will complete my studies. I am happy, and I think full of an energy, of an energy I had despaired of. It seems to me that I have found what I wanted. When I try to put it all into a phrase I say, "Man can embody truth but he cannot know it." I must embody it in the completion of my life.[2]

The alternatives of Baudelaire, of the romantic artist generally, are thus evaded. Objective knowledge and personal expression become identified so that the man disappears into his total apprehension of reality: expression is a part of study, study is the process of experience, poetry is the stabilized (embodied) process, truth. It is still necessary for the poet to assume that his experience is symbolic, that he is to a large extent a privileged being, but he is freed of the burden of egotism. The origin of knowledge is not in the poet but in the poem, which he must consult for knowledge.

Yeats distrusted the contemplation of one's own passivity and personal tragedy and sought instead an activity, of mind or of whole being, that would allow art and life to attain ". . . swiftness, volume, unity."[3] Hence the self-parasitic introspection of a Baudelaire or Clough cannot be justified, the self-absorption that Lawrence so despised is placed beyond the pale, and the remorse that characterizes so much of nineteenth-century literature becomes pointless. (Remorse, Claudel said, was the sole emotion that the nineteenth century could entertain with sincerity.)[4] Remorse appears in Yeats's poetry more as irritation or biographical fact, objective (I was unkind, I did this or that), rather than subjective tone. The concept of truth as dramatic event and poetry as an action embodying truth serves to externalize knowledge, separate it from person, so that knowledge of world or self is genuinely selfless. It is a gift, and like grace it gets no sanctification from the person on whom it descends.

This final articulation came at the close of a life of thought on the subject and was arrived at only after much doubt and conflict. Yeats came to realize that through his action as poet he had been able to approximate true knowledge of the self and the other, partly in the process of writing and consequent revelation but mainly because the poem once completed allowed him to contemplate, permanently shaped, the symbolic design of his experience. His intense scrutiny of poems as they formed in manuscript and appeared in printed books allowed him to realize his destiny in mass and outline. To compose a poem was literally to compose his soul.

Thus the motives that Baudelaire saw as mutually exclusive could be merged, that of making (articulating, fabricating) and that of expression (self-revelation). The so often noted re-imagining and rewriting of Yeats's poems came not only from a desire for aesthetic perfection but from a need for discovering what he had there embodied, with the hope that he might then establish in his own mind his destined truth and identity. Aesthetic perfection and truth were indistinguishable. Knowledge, making, and expression were identified. He spoke what until speaking he had not known, and he recorded his speech in order to learn.

He evaded the cruder mistakes possible in the position of the Romantic writer, but he remained to the very end intransigently, in his own term, one of the "last Romantics." The accomplishment of his work makes one wonder whether he did not really liberate potentialities elsewhere crippled or obscured in the current of poetic ideas since Goethe. His chief legacy to us may be a revitalized romanticism, aware fully of its weaknesses, incorporating what is vital in the negative criticism of the neoclassicist theorists, and at the same time remaining fully established in the spiritual conditions that mark our era and seem ever more pressing. His convictions on the nature of the poet form an extensive definition of the poet's role that, in its details and ramifications, is a major theoretical achievement.

In the remainder of this chapter I shall examine first Yeats's reaction to the modern concept of the artist's relation to his artifact and second the various aspects of his own theory, its relation to his social and religious thought and to the practice of his verse. In discussing the modernist attitude I stress the ideas of Pound and Eliot, not only because of their great prestige and influence but also because Yeats took his friend and antagonist Ezra Pound as a prototype of a newly emerging art that was the antithesis to his own and to the art he prized.

Yeats and Modernity

That Yeats should have been baffled by or indifferent to most visual art of the twentieth century is understandable. The clean academic figure drawing by him in the Irish National Gallery, his father's Titianesque portraits, his affection for the painting of Gustave Moreau, his hostility even to Manet and other Impressionists, let alone the Post-Impressionist, cubist, and abstract painters—all this bears witness to his acceptance of the most conservative criteria of nineteenth-century painting. Ezra Pound might argue for Wyndham Lewis, Brancusi, Gaudier-Brzeska, but when momentarily free

of that brilliant presence, Yeats returned to his early
and continued fondness for Pre-Raphaelitism:

> Two days ago [*ca.* 1913] I was at the Tate Gallery to see
> the early Millais's, and before his *Ophelia* as before the *Mary
> Magdalene and Mary of Galilee* of Rossetti that hung near, I
> recovered an old emotion. I forgot the art criticism of friends and
> saw wonderful, sad, happy people, moving through the scenery
> of my dreams.[5]

In poetry, too, as the *Oxford Book of Modern Verse*
notoriously testifies, he remained bound in affectionate
loyalty to his contemporaries of the 1890's. His comments on Eliot are cold, those on Pound ambiguous at
best, and no poetry at the center of experimentalism
draws his unqualified praise.

In part this hostility to the new art of the twentieth
century might be dismissed as a natural biographical
design. A poet's capacity for "appreciation" of new
work or for discrimination between various poems following out a process remote from his own interests is
not endless, and to most people modern art or poetry
means "the poets or artists current in my youth." Or one
might ascribe Yeats's indifference to modern art to the
provincialism of Dublin intellectual life or to his own
literal increasing blindness. All this might be conceded,
yet a doubt remains. For Yeats was given every opportunity to know the new art, and through Pound he
heard its motives and theories developed at length. His
refusal came not out of ignorance but out of principle.
He felt his deepest aesthetic convictions violated.

Perhaps his reaction will be made more intelligible
when seen against the background of ideas provided by
Ortega y Gasset's well-known essay on "The Dehumanization of Art." It appeared first in 1925, and—as Joseph

Frank has remarked [6]—it crystallized certain ideas with
brilliant cogency. Much of its impact comes from an
undercurrent of bitter reluctance, for Ortega was chron-
icling a series of events in art history with which he had
limited sympathy. Thus he has special pertinence in this
discussion because he represents what there was, in
the theory and practice of art from about 1908 to 1924,
that would strike the sensitive observer relatively detached from the arts by being a nonparticipant in the
creative process and by his deep immersion in the preceding culture.

In describing the new art, Ortega stresses those elements that mark a distinct deviation from the humanist
tradition of the Renaissance, and more specifically those
that break the continuity between nineteenth and twentieth century. The desire to purify art of all non-
artistic elements he sees as seminal. Growing from that
central idea are a strict will toward being antipopular
and a tendency toward "dehumanization":

> Such a tendency would effect a progressive elimination of
> the human, all too human, elements predominant in romantic
> and naturalistic production. And in this process a point can be
> reached in which the human content has grown so thin that it
> is negligible.[7]

This art provides no common area of reference between
artist and audience. Eliminating human forms, all reference to natural objects, eliminates also the audience
that responds to art as representation of nature. The vir-
tues of art so oriented, Ortega implies, are perceptible
only to persons of artistic training and sensibility.

Artist becomes blocked off from nonartist, and the

realm of art increasingly demarcated from nature.
When the artist has no allegiance to visible nature outside the art work, he can ultimately divorce the art work
even from his own feelings, so that his only responsibility is to the "scrupulous realization of the artifact."
His chief loyalty is then to the inherent nature of his
medium, its possibilities as indicator of color and form.
The Giottos at Padua, Matisse argued, make their impact not because of the prestige of their subject matter
but through their disposition of pigment, the sensible
surface of shape and tone. By now this complex of ideas
is so familiar that no one thinks it odd or precious to
consider a painting, as Maurice Denis urged, as
". . . essentially a plane surface covered by colors arranged in a certain order," [8] and Whistler's indifference
to the past, present, or future of a figure needed to provide a required black area would rouse no indignation
in any art school that I have heard of recently. For if
one accepts the point of view ascribed to modern artists
by Ortega, art should be considered completely apart
from subject matter. Far from painting "wonderful, sad,
happy people" moving through the scenery of his
dreams, Matisse imagined an ideal of art without subject:

> What I dream of is an art of equilibrium, purity, and tran-
> quillity, without disquieting or disturbing subjects, which could
> be for the mental worker, the business man, and the man of
> letters too, for example, a mental refreshment and relaxation,
> something analogous to a good easy chair in which one rests
> from his physical fatigue.[9]

A kind of sunny impudence marks this passage, a booby
trap for the solemn. The same sportive seriousness

marks Apollinaire's argument against natural representation:

> Les vertus plastiques: la pureté, l'unité et la vérité maintien-
> nent sous leurs pieds la nature terrassée.
> ⟋ . . . trop d'artistes-peintres adorent encore les plantes, les
> pierres, l'onde ou les hommes. . . .
> On laisse les ouvriers maîtriser l'univers et les jardiniers ont
> moins de respect pour la nature que n'en ont les artistes.
> Il est temps d'être les maîtres.[10]

But under all the guying, which is largely an attempt to
smoke out the opposition of fools, rests a serious substratum, an attack on pretense and inflation, that asks
for art a position of special distinction and privilege.

Ortega was taken in by this tone and assumed that
the new art looked on its processes as purely play. In
fact, he was witnessing a phase, a cutting back to ele-
mentals that had been crusted over by the accumula-
tions of a dead tradition. Matisse, after all, was Moreau's
student even more than Pound was Yeats's. To insist
on play, after the seriousness of Delacroix and Hugo,
those two great roadblocks in French culture, and the
massive accomplishments of the Impressionists, was
healthy and remedial. And against the slavish devotion
to the processes of nature that produced the haystack
paintings of Monet, what pleasure to turn toward the
possibilities of the medium and the liberated inventive-
ness of the spirit.

The stress on medium as distinct from nature attempted to evade the problem of the romantic artist by
simply ignoring the question of personality. The artist
was technician, practical joker, or agent who with detachment shaped artifacts pertinent to his experience of
his medium. In literary art, an analogous coolness,

Ortega thought, led to the sense of poetry as "the higher algebra of metaphor." Paul Valéry tells an anecdote that unites the two arts:

The great painter Degas often repeated to me a very true and simple remark by Mallarmé. Degas occasionally wrote verses, and some of those he left were delightful. But he often found great difficulty in this work accessory to his painting. (He was, by the way, the kind of man who would bring all possible difficulty to any art whatever.) One day he said to Mallarmé: "Yours is a hellish craft. I can't manage to say what I want, and yet I'm full of ideas. . . ." And Mallarmé answered: "My dear Degas, one does not make poetry with ideas, but with *words*." [11]

Degas was motivated by the simple aim of sincerity: expressing his ideas; Mallarmé by a professional aim: the construction of a verbal artifact.

In the criticism of Pound and Eliot, "personal sincerity" became as great a villain as was "natural representation" to Gleizes, Kandinsky, Matisse, Apollinaire. The "antipopularity" that Ortega saw as primary to their art was not a desire to *épater le bourgeois* but a will toward a new design of life predicated on art. It was corrective and pedagogical, directed against a prevailing aesthetic and in favor of one pertinent to the newly emerging art. In many respects it was a theory limited by time and by its targets.

When Eliot, for example, said that "The progress of an artist is a continual self-sacrifice, a continual extinction of personality," [12] he was writing directly to an intellectual milieu that took seriously opinions that identified artist and achievement:

I have found by spontaneous experience more and more that even the aesthetic pleasure of a poem depends for me on the fineness of the personality glimpsed between its lines; on the spirit of which the body of a book is inevitably the echo and the mould.[13]

Eliot had too much respect for the poetic line to waste his energy in looking at blank spaces on a page. He had every reason for being infuriated by the pompous platitudes of Henry Newbolt or John Middleton Murry:

> To know a work of literature is to know the soul of the man who created it, and who created it in order that his soul should be known.[14]

It was out of such irritation that he wrote his preface to Valéry's *Le Serpent:*

> To English amateurs, rather inclined to dismiss poetry which appears reticent, and to peer lasciviously between the lines for biographical confession, such an activity [as Valéry's] may seem no other than a *jeu de quilles*. . . . To reduce one's disorderly and mostly silly personality to the gravity of a *jeu de quilles* would be to do an excellent thing: yet for this a great poet, Landor, has been condemned to obloquy. And we forget that Browning, and Shelley, and Byron, for all their effervescence, give us less of themselves than does Turgenev or Flaubert. And perhaps the reticence of Villon is no less than that of Valéry. One is prepared for art when one has ceased to be interested in one's own emotions and experiences except as material; and when one has reached this point of indifference one will pick and choose according to very different principles from the principles of those people who are still excited by their own feelings and passionately enthusiastic over their own passions. And observe that, as M. Thibaudet well says, "Valéry's interest in "technique" is something much more comprehensive than an interest in the skilful disposition of words for their own sake: it is a recognition of the truth that not our feelings, but the pattern which we may make of our feelings, is the centre of value.[15]

In this brief note and in his celebrated essay on "Tradition and the Individual Talent," Eliot expressed his impatience with a notion of personality developed during the Romantic period, compromised by the Victorians and brought to ripeness by the Pre-Raphaelites, especially by Pater and Symons. Eliot's arguments for tradition, his insistence that a poet is often at his best when the voices of his predecessors are most clearly heard in his art, the substitution of the medium of poetry (language, objective correlatives) for the poet as personality—these were antidote to what Eliot saw as poisonous errors in the immediate past. He inverts the terms of Pater and Symons; their good becomes Eliot's evil, their evil his good. With an eye on the presuppositions of his elder contemporaries, Eliot says, ". . . the more perfect the artist, the more completely separate in him will be the man who suffers and the mind which creates. . . ." [16] The man passively undergoes, the mind shapes and forms.

Implied in this poetics is a hierarchy of values in which the man's total responses are suspect unless disciplined by traditional intellect. The medium of poetry is the body of received linguistic forms and possibilities, out of which may be shaped artifacts not necessarily related directly to the man's experience. The assumption is that the artifact will be considerably better than the experience because less subject to the flaws inherent in individual men: it will be redeemed. Personal experience has the same relation to poetic art that natural form does to visual art: it is the occasion, the pretext. It plays no part in the final text. Art rectifies life.

Pound's poetics, though in many ways close to Eliot's, is not limited by this essentially religious conservatism. Seeing and feeling, far from being the occasion, are the ultimate justification of the artist's treatment of the medium. And the medium is more narrowly conceived, as image rather than language:

> The painters realise that what matters is form and colour. Musicians long ago learned that programme music was not the ultimate music. . . .
>
> The Image is the poet's pigment. The painter should use his colour because he sees it or feels it. I don't much care whether he is representative or non-representative. He should depend, of course, on the creative, not upon the mimetic or representational part in his work. It is the same in writing poems, the author must use his image because he sees it or feels it, not because he thinks he can use it to back up some creed or some system of ethics or economics.[17]

Pound moves one step beyond Eliot, for he not only asks that literary art be in no way dependent on the experience of its writer, but he insists that it should be committed to no creed or system of thought. Analyzing his own development, Pound described it as a process of depersonalization:

> I began this search for the real in a book called *Personae*, casting off, as it were, complete masks of the self in each poem. I continued in long series of translations, which were but more elaborate masks.
>
> Secondly, I made poems like "The Return," which is an objective reality and has a complicated sort of significance, like Mr. Epstein's "Sun God," or Mr. Brzeska's "Boy with a Coney." Thirdly, I have written "Heather," which represents a state of consciousness, or "implies," or "implicates" it.[18]

His approving description of a response to "Heather" underlines the impersonality of the poems:

> A Russian correspondent, after having called it ["Heather"] a symbolist poem, and having been convinced that it was not

symbolism, said slowly: "I see, you wish to give people new eyes, not to make them see some new particular thing."

These two latter sorts of poems ["The Return" and "Heather"] are impersonal, and that fact brings us back to what I said about absolute metaphor. They are Imagisme, and in so far as they are Imagisme, they fall in with the new sculpture.[19]

"Absolute" metaphor is impersonal, and in Pound's terminology "absolute" here means "appropriate." Implied in his theory of the Image is a concept of decorum, not as social or linguistic rectitude but as poetic accuracy. Pound was impatient of vague associations, and his desire for the hard, limited outline fortified his distrust of references to the unknowable and irrelevant personality of the author. Such references were sentimental: they asked a response in excess of the actual presentative effectiveness of the medium. For the same reason he objected to icons requiring the support of a symbolic system for their power:

Imagisme is not symbolism. The symbolists dealt in "association," that is, in a sort of allusion, almost of allegory. They degraded the symbol to the status of a word. They made it a form of metonymy. One can be grossly "symbolic," for example, by using the term "cross" to mean "trial." The symbolist's *symbols* have a fixed value, like numbers in arithmetic, like 1, 2, and 7. The imagiste's images have a variable significance, like the signs *a*, *b*, and *x* in algebra.

Moreover, one does not want to be called a symbolist, because symbolism has usually been associated with mushy technique.[20]

The arithmetical system of, say, Christianity or Neo-Platonism was in poetry a mode of cheating: it asked a uniform response, whatever context was provided for the symbol. To Pound, however, the value of an image came from the quality and range of the context it realized. Art was not the expression of meaning and order; it was the basis.

The record of Yeats's quarrel with aspects of the modern aesthetic (especially as presented to him by Pound) is far from complete, but his central objections are clear. He could not accept the idea that subject made no difference to the value of a poem, that medium was all. In the only recently published preface to his collected essays, he writes of the necessity of a dignified and noble subject matter:

> I have never said clearly that I condemn all that is not tradition, that there is a subject-matter which has descended like that "deposit" certain philosophers speak of. At the end of his essay upon "Style" Pater says that a book written according to the principles he has laid down will be well written, but whether it is a great book or not depends upon subject-matter. This subject matter is something I have received from the generations, part of that compact with my fellow-men made in my name before I was born. I cannot break from it without breaking from some part of my own nature; and sometimes it has come to me in supernormal experience; I have met with ancient myths in my dreams, brightly lit; and I think it allied to the wisdom or instinct that guides a migratory bird.[21]

And the complete separation of maker from artifact he found not only impossible but undesirable. After a quarrel with Pound, he won the argument by the expedient of speaking to his notebook:

> The one reason for putting our actual situation into our art is that the struggle for complete affirmation may be, often must be, that art's chief poignancy. I must, though [the] world shriek at me, admit no act beyond my power, nor thing beyond my knowledge, yet because my divinity is far off I blanch and tremble.[22]

Yeats's position, then, was in important respects radically deviant from the by now conventional attitude toward the relation between poet and poem. At the same time he did not deny the insights won by adherents to the concept of art as impersonal, so that his views complement and extend those of Valéry, Pound, Eliot. The autobiographical element that Valéry saw as regrettable impurity was to Yeats opportunity and challenge. Far from denying his social role, he attempted to transform his immediate audience. He did not think of his personality as nonessential to his art, and he built a coherent and unified philosophy so that his poems present a continuity of interlocking symbolic forms. He justified his procedures in the personal experience of his *Autobiography* and in the symbolic structures of *A Vision,* as well as in his letters, notebooks, and—above all—his poems.

In the poems, he very deliberately refused to accept any single mode of treating the drama of his experience. A part of his attractiveness resides in the multiple surface of his work, not merely the levels of meaning within any single poem but the several distinct modes of rendering experience that he accepted as normal possibilities in shaping poetry. His relation to his subject matter, as has been often remarked, allows for the validity of multiple, even logically incompatible, attitudes, and these attitudes were expressible through multiple dramatic techniques that may be, on the surface, contradictory, but that were in fact compatible in his comprehensive dramaturgy.

The classic locus for this multiplicity is the series of poems occasioned by the death of Major Robert Gregory, one treating the death from the airman's stoic point of view, another discussing his death in a pastoral dialogue strangely wedded to theosophic beliefs, the third a political attack on the hypocrisy of the British, the last the great human monologue, "In Memory of Major Robert Gregory." [23] The poems vary in technique as much as in attitude. Written when Yeats was coming to the height of his powers, each poem places the poet at a different distance from his subject, from the personal reminiscence and self-dramatizing of "In Memory of Major Robert Gregory" to the austere dramatis persona of "An Irish Airman Foresees His Death." They suggest the range, the comprehensiveness, of his mature poetics, from the most deeply personal to the impersonal, from undisguised self to disconnected though always admired personae.

The "Major Gregory" poems were written at the beginning of the great creative period that dated from his marriage through *The Tower* to the *Last Poems*. They appeared at the very time that Pound and Eliot were phrasing most cogently their arguments against the complacent romanticism of their elder contemporaries. They show, as do his letters to his father from 1909 to 1916, Yeats's deep involvement in the poetics of his own youth, the era of Pater and Symons. Writing to his father, Yeats identified an intimate poetry with life and experience and argued for the importance of personal sincerity. Answering his father's request that he suggest an analogue in poetry to "imitation" of nature in painting, he continued his argument with Ezra Pound (an advocate of Wyndham Lewis), by identifying the abstract in painting with the rhetorical in poetry:

I suggest that the corresponding things are drama and the pictorial element and that in poetry those who lack these are rhetoricians. I feel in Wyndham Lewis's Cubist pictures an ele-

ment corresponding to rhetoric arising from his confusion of
the abstract with the rhythmical. Rhythm implies a living body,
a breast to rise and fall, or limbs that dance, while the abstract
is incompatible with life. The Cubist is abstract.[24]

The "rhythm" that he here discusses is identified with
conscious feeling, and it is the essential voice of the
speaker or artist:

I separate the rhythmical and the abstract. They are brothers
but one is Abel and one is Cain. In poetry they are not confused
for we know that poetry is rhythm, but in music-hall verses we
find an abstract cadence, which is vulgar because it is apart
from imitation. This cadence is a mechanism, it never suggests
a voice shaken with joy or sorrow as poetical rhythm does. It is
but the noise of a machine and not the coming and going of the
breath.[25]

Without this rhythm and without the reference to actual experience, a writer like Carlyle became "Insincere
and theatrical. . . ." When he reflected on "Contemporary Poetry" in preparation for a lecture, Yeats
considered Ernest Dowson and Lionel Johnson as representative of the poets in the Rhymers' Club:

The doctrine of that group, or rather of the majority of it, was
that lyric poetry should be personal. That a man should express
his life and do this without shame or fear. Ernest Dowson did
this and became a most extraordinary poet, one feels the pressure
of his life behind every line as if he were a character in a play
of Shakespeare's. Johnson had no theories of any sort but came
to do much the same through the example of Dowson and others
and because his life grew gradually so tragic that it filled his
thoughts.[26]

But the "pressure of his life" was something separate
from the actual social being that he presented. Yeats
was as aware as anyone of the absurdity of Dowson's

ludicrous passion for a waitress, but that socially foolish activity was merely an occasion that allowed him to release passion that, in his poetry, received an objective validation. He was comparable to ". . . Byron in *Manfred* or Forbes-Robertson in a romantic part," in the sense that these personages ". . . have all personality but we do not necessarily know much about their characters. . . ." [27]

The peculiar vocabulary here used has caused a great deal of confusion. The distinction between character on the one hand and personality or passion on the other is a distinction that Yeats had developed in his contemplation of the problems of the theater. "Character" he identified with the social creature, the being that we see on the street and consult on professional or business problems, the mechanical creature of social institutions and customs. "Personality" was asocial and even antisocial, the reality that underlay and could be antithetical to "character." He identified character with rhetorical form and abstraction, and when he sought an escape from this living death he found it in "personal expression": "The escape is personal expression, or drama. But this personal expression must not become characterization nor in poetry can drama itself become chiefly characterization. In personal expression characterization is egotism." [28]

The paradox involved in this formulation was steadily at the center of his thought on the relation between art and experience. How to be personal and yet avoid egotism? How to get the pressure of his life behind every line without presenting himself as a pompous idealization? The answer lay not in any single neat theory but in the process of dramatic revelation, with many false starts and struggles toward "complete affirmation." Meditating on this set of problems through his long productive life, he saw the human being in three categories: that of individuality, in which the being refused both social function and his passionate role in the structure of the universe; that of character, in which the being refused his larger responsibilities in the interests of the safe, the defined, the abstract; and finally, that of personality, in which the being accepted his passionate function in the great universal drama. These categories were means of assessing activity, and they were also the burden and fate of any being. They were, in effect, to define the range and motive of his own poetry, so that— as in the Major Gregory poems—he moved from personal reminiscence through a definition of Gregory's social role to an embodiment of Gregory's passionate function. Present constantly to his mind was a feeling for, a drive toward, a sense of the world as a dramatic construct in which each man sought a role, given or invented, that would allow the fullest currency of passion.

Toward the close of his life, in the only recently published introduction to a projected new collection of his poems, he managed to phrase his sense of the poetic fate, as—in his last letter—he had phrased his personal fate:

A poet writes always out of his personal life, in his finest works out of its tragedy, whatever it be, remorse, lost love, or mere loneliness; he never speaks directly as to someone at a breakfast table, there is always a phantasmagoria . . . even when the poet seems most himself . . . he is never the bundle of accident and

incoherence that sits down to breakfast; he has been re-born as
an idea, something intended, complete . . . he is more type
than man, more passion than type. . . . He is part one of his
phantasmagoria and we adore him because nature has grown intelligible, and by so doing a part of our creative power.[29]

When a man spoke as a poet, he was transmuted by his
participation in an older and more inclusive community so that he was at once a person and a passion:
he was not a "character" and he was hardly to be considered an "individuality." He was adorable not because
he was ingratiating, engaging, a nice man but because, to return to our earlier consideration of Baudelaire, he spoke what we do not dare confess. His daring
was the source of his charm, and his charm was at once
magical and tragic, ". . . more type than man, more
passion than type." He released nature by making it intelligible and ". . . a part of our creative power."

Yeats moved toward this final definition with hesitation and trouble. I should like now to consider the
formulation that he arrived at in writing his *Autobiography*, especially the parts he wrote between 1914
and 1922 when he was establishing in his own mind his
mature sense of the poetic genius. His own life could
not be presented in any frank completeness, and he
was confined to an analysis of his past (and veiled)
conduct and the lives and works of his friends. Since so
many of the chief figures of his own life were alive,
sensitive, and vocal, his autobiography was limited to
the drawing of his soul rather than his full accidental
being, and in tracing the lineaments of his poetic being
he could use the figures of William Morris, Henley, and
—since his politics were a form of poetics—O'Leary.

Writing to one of the major personages of his life, Olivia Shakespear, he sketched a design that shows how great his omissions were:

I send Four Years which is the first third of the complete memoirs. As they go on they will grow less personal, or at least less adequate as personal representation, for the most vehement part of youth must be left out, the only part that one well remembers and lives over again in memory when one is in old age, the paramount part. I think this will give all the more sense of inadequateness from the fact that I study every man I meet at some moment of crisis—I alone have no crisis.[30]

His studies of critical moments in the lives of others were genuine self-analyses. Meeting his various friends at their moments of crisis, he could establish through their reactions a concept of valued human quality. They would be metaphors on which to base his own sense of poetic function.

Like many autobiographies, this book makes Yeats more passive than in fact he was, shows him as interested observer rather than eager and agonized participant. The book observes the fiction that Yeats was a learner rather than mover, a convention that the autobiographical genre has always exploited, most obviously in the examples of St. Augustine and Henry Adams. For this reason it is dangerous to take literally the substance of any given passage of the text. The book explores various hypothetical possibilities about the poet's nature, each of which is provisional and tentative. From this process emerge a series of related roles that the poet may, in his practice, at one moment or another assume, a dramaturgy at once coherent and various but never absolute. It is part of the retrospective (and fictional)

structure of Yeats's book that at each moment he should
seem completely persuaded of the efficacy of the dramaturgy then at stake. He relies on our good sophisticated
sense to evaluate the several moments in their relation
to the total theoretical design.

The most rudimentary element of his poetic dramaturgy came from his father, who stressed the dramatic
element in poetry. J. B. Yeats disliked any "speculative"
element in poetry and admired work concerned with
passionate moments that forbade by their ecstatic intensity any hint of generalization or abstraction. Reading
lyric poems he sought ". . . some actual man" so that
he could see ". . . the lineaments of some desirable,
familiar life." [31] The actual man would rebuke the
abstract and embody an ideal for the affections:
". . . All must be an idealisation of speech, and at some
moment of passionate action or somnambulistic rev-
ery." [32] He exalted dramatic poetry above all kinds, and
to his mind the lyric—with the weight of the person
in each line—was a form of drama.

Even in J. B. Yeats's phrasing of the concept of
dramatic personal utterance, there were certain reser-
vations, and Yeats himself—although he acknowledged
the importance of his father's ideas in his development
—saw that personal utterance had some of the artifici-
ality of pose:

I was about to learn that if a man is to write lyric poetry he must
be shaped by nature and art to some one out of half a dozen
traditional poses, and be lover or saint, sage or sensualist, or
mere mocker of all life; and that none but that stroke of luckless
luck can open before him the accumulated expression of the
world.[33]

As the pattern of his career would emerge, he was to accept not one but half a dozen traditional poses, and his participation in the "accumulated expression of the world" was to be richer and more various than this statement would suggest. Early in his life he carried the implications of this position farther than even J. B. Yeats was willing to go, so that "I was soon to vex my father by defining truth as 'the dramatically appropriate utterance of the highest man. . . .' " [34]

Such refinements of the concept of personal utterance came later, however; in his early years he applied the concept so literally that he found himself sentimentally accepting bad writing that expressed feelings evoking in him an analogous loyalty. When he read some verses describing the Irish shore as seen by a returning dying emigrant, his eyes filled with tears in spite of revulsion against the texture of the poem. And when he found that the verses were by a political exile whose life had ended virtually with his return to Ireland, he decided that they had moved him because ". . . they contained the actual thoughts of a man at a passionate moment of life. . . ." From such examples and from the general tone of late nineteenth-century poetic theory he moved to a formulation that personal utterance was as valid as objective drama. Time and again in speaking of poetry he returned to the metaphor of stage drama, and the metaphor was so firmly implanted in his mind that it colored all his thought:

We should write out our own thoughts in as nearly as possible the language we thought them in, as though in a letter to an intimate friend. We should not disguise them in any way; for our lives give them force as the lives of people in plays give force to their words. Personal utterance, which had almost ceased in English literature, could be as fine an escape from rhetoric and abstraction as drama itself. . . . I tried from that on to write out of my emotions exactly as they came to me in life, not changing them to make them more beautiful.[35]

His formulation, in spite of the dramatic overtone, could serve as an example of the personalism that, as we have seen, so irritated Eliot by its encouragement of lascivious peering between the lines. In Yeats's early thought, the poet was to be a man who sincerely expressed his interesting life, so that he might make an intimate appeal of soul to soul:

"If I can be sincere and make my language natural, and without becoming discursive, like a novelist, and so indiscreet and prosaic," I said to myself, "I shall, if good luck or bad luck make my life interesting, be a great poet; for it will be no longer a matter of literature at all." Yet when I re-read those early poems which gave me so much trouble, I find little but romantic convention, unconscious drama. It is so many years before one can believe enough in what one feels even to know what the feeling is.

His concern with personal dramatic utterance was so persistent that one critic has called the entire body of his poetry a set of marginalia on his autobiography.[36] Yeats came from a generation that, as he said in the preface to *The Trembling of the Veil,* valued "personality," so that he wrote of his friends: "They were artists and writers and certain among them men of genius, and the life of a man of genius, because of his greater sincerity, is often an experiment that needs analysis and record. At least my generation so valued personality that it thought so." [37] It was, ironically, in his thought upon those very figures that he expressed one of his major correctives to a poetics that identified value with sincerity and personality.

The simple identification of person and poet changed radically as he contemplated Henley and Morris. He thought of Henley as a man unconsciously fulfilling a role large in suggestion, much grander than Henley knew, and close to the realization of an ideal type, giving an individual form to "our passions." His poems were not adequate, but a reality came through them that, as in the verses of the Irish exile, redeemed a banal surface:

I used to say when I spoke of his poems: 'He is like a great actor with a bad part; yet who would look at Hamlet in the grave scene if Salvini played the grave-digger?' and I might so have explained much that he said and did. I meant that he was like a great actor of passion . . . and an actor of passion will display some one quality of soul, personified again and again, just as a great poetical painter, Titian, Botticelli, Rossetti, may depend for his greatness upon a type of beauty which presently we call by his name.[38]

In active discourse also, Henley was a dramatis persona, his opinions emanating from an unconscious will toward converting a drawing room into a stage. He truculently sought opponents in order to play his role, so that he could ". . . bring life to the dramatic crisis and expression to that point of artifice where the true self could find its tongue." [39] Yeats here moves in the direction earlier indicated by his sense of traditional "pose" and "role," the products of dramatic "artifice." The true self is evidently something deeper than the immediate social presence.

The "true self" was not only different from—it was
even opposite to—the actual visible being; it was a construct that could be "built up": "Henley, half inarticu-
late . . . beset with personal quarrels, built up an
image of power and magnanimity till it became, at
moments, when seen as it were by lightning, his true
self." [40]

Henley thus became an emblem of the artist, a being
whose life projected a persona that embodied a complex of aesthetic forms that were frequently the opposite of his public character or private self. He was the
center of a personifying passion that allowed him to
adopt a role and thus unlock a range of expression quite
separate from his biological or social condition. Service
of this role was service of the personal genius and ac-
counted for the contrasts that Yeats saw in a being so
unified as that of William Morris. He did not, in his
maturity, see great value in Morris's poetry, ". . . and
yet, if some angel offered me the choice, I would choose
to live his life, poetry and all, rather than my own or
any other man's." [41] Yeats's admiration of Morris grew
from his persuasion that Morris had discovered and followed his genius, so that he had attained a deeply unified moral and intellectual simplicity:

> The dream world of Morris was as much the antithesis of daily
> life as with other men of genius, but he was never conscious of
> the antithesis and so knew nothing of intellectual suffering. His
> intellect, unexhausted by speculation or casuistry, was wholly
> at the service of hand and eye, and whatever he pleased he did
> with an unheard-of ease and simplicity, and if style and vo-
> cabulary were at times monotonous, he could not have made
> them otherwise without ceasing to be himself. [42]

The term "himself" is here being used to indicate an entity remote from the strong, irascible, joyful, blundering man that Yeats describes with such economical clarity in succeeding sentences. The "self" projected in Morris's poetry was not even a personified idea:

He did not project like Henley or like Wilde, an image of himself, because having all his imagination set upon making and doing he had little self-knowledge. He imagined instead new conditions of making and doing. . . .[43]

The identification of artist and work here changes to an identification of the artist's work with the artist's dream. The dream expresses the artist's deepest self, his genius or daimon that allows him participation in the permanent life of the living and the dead, that timeless and spaceless community of spirits that Yeats thought of as reality. The artist who attains self-expression by reaching ". . . that point of artifice where the true self could find its tongue" [44] is conducting an enterprise unlike the simple personalism of, say, Tennyson or Arnold; he is seeking to liberate some reality much deeper than his experiences at school or the loss of a friend. Yeats was fond of quoting Verlaine's stricture on "In Memoriam"—"when he should have been broken-hearted, he had many reminiscences" [45]—and in certain humors he despised the mere untransmuted personal experience offered as poetic with as much vehemence as he hated mechanical rhetoric. What he admired in the life and work of Morris was not their simple one to one correlation—this he overtly denied— but the fact that each of the two, life and letters, pursued completely distinct but equally fluent and uninterrupted courses, each a unity, each separate, and this cleavage made endurable by a simple unreflecting acceptance. In the last analysis what he envied in Morris comes very close to being simple-mindedness.

For Yeats, such freedom from intellectual suffering as he ascribed to Morris was impossible. He might desire an "unpremeditated joyous energy" that would come out of him easily and return into the experience of Connacht—one of his permanent norms—naturally, but this would be qualified by the vestiges of personality that he found in even the most selfless of medieval craftsmen and made ultimately impossible by Yeats's participation in ". . . that sterile modern complication . . . my originality. . . ." [46] He might admire Morris and the remembered traditional artists of the Middle Ages, their simple untroubled spontaneity of vision and assertion, but he found himself also bound to the fate of the tragic generation—Dowson, Lionel Johnson, Beardsley—and their immersion in the modern malady of the sickened and divided self:

> What portion in the world can the artist have
> Who has awakened from the common dream
> But dissipation and despair? [47]

In these writers, and in himself, he could see the penalties of living in a world without any received convention more viable than the low dream of an increasingly commercial civilization. Forced to construct a significant world out of their own subjective lives, they could get only formal comfort from Christianity:

. . . what can the Christian confessor say to those who more and more must make all out of the privacy of their thought, call-

ing up perpetual images for desire, for he cannot say "Cease to
be artist, cease to be poet," when the whole life is art and poetry,
nor can he bid men leave the world, who suffer from the terrors
that pass before shut eyes.[48]

Eager as Yeats was for a community of spirit in which
the poet would find a natural place, he could not pretend that his present world provided those conditions.
In spite of his dislike of originality or individuality and
the attendant meditative modes of constructing in verse
a "view" of the world ("I hated and I still hate with an
ever growing hatred the literature of the point of
view"),[49] he found himself compelled to write a considerable body of didactic and satiric poems, explana-
tory and critical prose, all wasteful. He delighted in
ages that granted the artist a fixed subject matter and
thus allowed him to work in a unified social order that
would include his art as part of an ecology, but in the
fragmented world of his actual experience, he could
only work toward such a condition, and without much
hope. His hatred of "abstraction," which seems excessive,[50] becomes intelligible when it is realized that it
was to Yeats not only a term describing a language
function but a term that implied the breakdown of
unity in the man and in the community, the isolation
of occupation from occupation and class from class. The
poet felt this fragmentation more immediately than the
lawyer or priest or peasant because his task was more
noticeably multiplied: he had no mode of communicat-
ing his vision to others, and he was forced into isolation
and frustration. He could cry out across the gulf of
separation in rage or he could sing in a vacuum, but
his work would in either instance suffer because it did

not express a natural community of feeling that, in turn, was in consonance with the structure of the universe. Such work could not represent the marriage of folk imagination and civilized intellect that Yeats saw in all great art and symbolized by the centaur. Lacking contact with a living community of spirit, poetry would drift into elaborate formalism, contrived by the intellect and lacking the substance of art that not only came out of an entire human concourse but returned to it with an invigorating force. He thought constantly of Homer and Dante and envied their achievement: not the creation of great artifacts but the articulation of heroic (superhuman) attitudes and feeling that could be widely shared and sung by ordinary men, so that their work actually exalted the experience of an entire world rather than pleasing only the aesthetic motives, however highly refined, of specialized sensibilities.

This motive, which radically differentiates his from the artist's motives as described by Ortega,[51] was strengthened by the unshaped image of reborn Ireland, where he could find in the incomparable cadre of eighteenth-century Dublin and in the still living folk imagination of the west, potentialities that might permit the emergence of a unified people with a common motive and design. The special blending of the aristocratic Protestant ascendancy with the complicated pagan–Christian folk Irish imagination that he proposed was no less monstrous than a centaur and about as probable in twentieth-century Eire. But Ireland had not yet settled into its present mold, and though his motives were to be disappointed in physical fact, the very presence of Ireland allowed him to project a com-

plete image of possible life on a limited area. It encouraged him also to keep a distance from that interna-
tional world of the arts which was a source of strength
but never an overwhelming influence on his work:

> Doubtless because fragments broke into even smaller frag-
> ments we saw one another in a light of bitter comedy, and in the
> arts, where now one technical element reigned and now another,
> generation hated generation, and accomplished beauty was
> snatched away when it had most engaged our affections.[52]

Against this fragmentation, the inconstancy of achievement, he could—largely through his verse—form an
image of possibility that would rouse the Irish to a full
articulation of their powers:

> Nations, races, and individual men are unified by an image,
> or bundle of related images, symbolical or evocative of the state
> of mind, which is of all states of mind not impossible, the most
> difficult to that man, race, or nation; because only the greatest
> obstacle that can be contemplated without despair, rouses the
> will to full intensity.[53]

For the gregarious bragging Irish, the image of possibility lonely, austere, and distinguished would serve
that need. And the time was ripe for a sudden fresh development in Ireland:

> . . . I had begun to hope, or to half hope, that we might be
> the first in Europe to seek unity as deliberately as it had been
> sought by theologian, poet, sculptor, architect, from the eleventh
> to the thirteenth century. Doubtless we must seek it differently,
> no longer considering it convenient to epitomise all human
> knowledge, but find it we well might could we first find philos-
> ophy and a little passion.[54]

He saw especially in the figure of John O'Leary a
heroic political emblem, a man who had accepted a role

not designed merely in order to please a crowd, isolated and integral:

> If we were, as I had dreaded, declamatory, loose and brag-
> ging, we were but the better fitted—that declared and measured
> —to create unyielding personality, manner at once cold and
> passionate, daring long premeditated act; and if bitter beyond
> all the people of the world, we might yet lie—that too declared
> and measured—nearest the honeyed comb. . . .[55]

Speaking of O'Leary, Yeats found in him a man that
had ". . . personality, a point of view not made for
the crowd's sake, but for self-expression. . . ."[56] His
point of view was in no way philosophical, for "He
had no philosophy, but things distressed his palate."
The practical efficacy of O'Leary never troubled Yeats.
He saw O'Leary as a figure for contemplation, an
integral and admirable being in his isolation and stoi-
cism. Qualities spoke through, and were embodied in,
O'Leary, as they were more fitfully and infrequently in
J. F. Taylor, O'Leary's follower. Because he scorned
and maintained his dignity against the practical world,
O'Leary could express fully his innate being. Yeats
found in this political hero a tragic personage analogous
to the poet: dignified, isolated, free, passionate, committed to an ideal of conduct above the low dream that
was taken for reality by bankers, schoolmasters, and
clergymen.

Thus in spite of the ideal of Ireland liberated in
polity and spirit, the implied norms of human conduct
that appear in the *Autobiography* are all eminently
antisocial. The kind of revolt that they imply is not a
mere revolt against social mores—Yeats's dislike of
bourgeois morality is so deep that it hardly requires

expression—but a revolt against the entire idea of character and personal function that those mores are based upon. Even the aim of so public an institution as the Abbey Theatre was revelation and transformation, an act of dramatic magic that would change its public as surely as would fighting at the barricades, and more deeply.

Implied in Yeats's dispute with his society was a belief in a condition of being—political, religious, artistic—that allowed the power of the whole man to enter freely into the entire society, the relation of wholeness being reciprocal. Since it was useless to pretend that this relation existed in the Ireland and England that he knew, a major function of the poet was not merely exalting the moments of life but transforming the conditions of human and social being. This was not the rage of the aesthete against the bourgeois unless we translate those terms into some view that will allow one to see bourgeois and aesthete as figures representing more than merely social designs. The issue was freedom of spirit, and the chief complication in its way was the multiplicity of divisions that afflicted the society and came to a clear focus in the condition of the artist. From Goethe on, a chief preoccupation of the major literary artists of Europe had been the divided self, and the series of astonishing fade-outs in English poetry from Wordsworth through Clough and Arnold to Swinburne merely dramatizes this terrible split in the human consciousness. Frank Kermode has suggested that Arnold stopped writing poetry to save his "soul," [57] and if one substitutes some less honorific terminology, Arnold's refusal is certainly a major defeat

in the history of the human spirit. Arnold withdrew in
the face of the poetic problems presented by the sense
of division within self and world. Yeats treated the
same problems fully, so that the main theme of his
poetry is the fragmented self and world, and their possible wholeness. And unlike Arnold, Yeats's work toward the transformation of life never betrayed his sense
of duty as poet, that is, of duty toward embodying and
portraying the exultant possibilities of integral man.
At the same time his awareness of the actual conditions of life compelled him to realize that the possibilities of experience were dual, that the simple exaltation
of experience was one main poetic function, but that
the other was a delineation of tragic limitation and
necessary failure. Exaltation and destruction were often
simultaneous, and if destruction was the price of exaltation, it was not too high a price.

The poet's function covers a wide range of possibility, from the direct expression of personal feeling
through satirical criticism to delineation of tragic historical circumstance to the embodiment of ideal passion. Two main ideas, however, underlie the rumina-
tions that Yeats made on the puzzling problem of the
relation between maker and artifact. The first idea is
that the poet established his personality by actions that
were in the most profound sense artificial: hence the
recurrence of such terms as "pose" or "role" or "artifice."
The process that allowed the poet to discover or reveal
his most basic reality was further complicated by the
social and historical designs of the modern era. The
second idea is that lyric poetry—and life itself—were

best understood as dramatic processes. The very universe was to be seen as a dramatic structure.

So Plotinus had understood the nature and function of human personality, and, although Yeats came to the dedicated study of Plotinus (in the Stephen MacKenna translation) late in life, he knew Plotinus early and the passage in the third *Ennead* on the drama and the soul articulates with more than coincidental fullness many of Yeats's implicit notions. As F. A. C. Wilson has argued, Yeats was in many important respects a Neo-Platonist, and the third *Ennead* is certainly closely related to the short poem "Whence Had They Come?"

> Eternity is passion, girl or boy
> Cry at the onset of the sexual joy
> 'For ever and for ever'; then awake
> Ignorant what Dramatis Personae spake;
> A passion-driven exultant man sings out
> Sentences that he has never thought;
> The Flagellant lashes those submissive loins
> Ignorant what that dramatist enjoins,
> What master made the lash. Whence had they come,
> The hand and lash that beat down frigid Rome?
> What sacred drama through her body heaved
> When world-transforming Charlemagne was conceived? [58]

The poet sees life (history) as the expression of destiny formed by some generally unknown dramatist, as does the beautiful passage in Plotinus:

> In the dramas of human art, the poet provides the words but the actors add their own quality, good or bad—for they have more to do than merely repeat the author's words—in the truer drama which dramatic genius imitates in its degree, the Soul displays itself in a part assigned by the creator of the piece. [59]

The problem of casting is taken care of by the great original dramatist, but the actor has to feel himself into the role and will succeed insofar as he comprehends and follows the grand motive:

> As the actors of our stages get their masks and costumes, robes of state or rags, so a Soul is allotted its fortunes, and not at haphazard but always under a Reason: it adapts itself to the fortunes assigned to it, attunes itself, arranges itself rightly to the drama, to the whole Principle of the peace: then it speaks out its business, exhibiting at the same time all that a Soul can express of its own quality, as a singer in a song. A voice, a bearing, naturally fine or vulgar, may increase the charm of a piece; on the other hand, an actor with his ugly voice may make a sorry exhibition of himself, yet the drama stands as good a work as ever: the dramatist taking the action which a sound criticism suggests, disgraces one, taking his part from him, with perfect justice: another man he promotes to more serious roles or to any more important play he may have, while the first is cast for whatever minor work there may be.[60]

The Soul also brings to its acting of its part certain personal excellences or defects and must accept a role "superimposed upon its own character and conduct" and act that role with appropriate dignity:

> Souls . . . act in a vaster place than any stage; the Author has made them masters of all this world; they have a wide choice of place; they themselves determine the honour or discredit in which they are agents since their place and part are in keeping with their quality: they therefore fit into the Reason-Principle of the Universe, each adjusted, most legitimately, to the appropriate environment, as every string of the lyre is set in the precisely right position, determined by the Principle directing musical utterance, for the due production of the tones within its capacity. All is just and good in the Universe in which every actor is set in his own quite appropriate place, though it be to utter in the

Darkness and in Tartarus the dreadful sounds whose utterance there is well.[61]

Whether in Hades or the Isles of the Blessed, the Soul is enjoined to audibility:

> This Universe is good not when the individual is a stone, but when everyone throws in his own voice towards a total harmony, singing out a life—thin, harsh, imperfect, though it be. The Syrinx does not utter merely one pure note; there is a thin obscure sound which blends in to make the harmony of Syrinx music: the harmony is made up from tones of various grades, all the tones differing, but the resultant of all forming one sound.
>
> . . . there is local difference, but from every position every string gives forth its own tone, the sound appropriate, at once, to its particular place and to the entire plan.[62]

This destined role, as Plotinus implies, can be at times superficially unfitting to the "character and conduct" of the individual, and it is the duty of the soul to fight its way free of accidents that keep it from fulfilling itself and the universal design.

So the poet's problem symbolizes the problem of every man, to discover his role, and if he lives in an age when the role of any being is not evident, he will suffer from confusion and waste in the process of finding his function. The admirable figures in the procession of Yeats's *Autobiography* are those, especially Morris and O'Leary, who have discovered the role that allows self-expression. But the self that Yeats wishes expressed is not the temporal individuality, nor does it necessarily have to do with the character and conduct of the man in a social world. Very few men enjoy the vigor and effectiveness that an identification of universal and social

role would grant, and the individuated character of the
man is not to be confused with his passionate personality.

Some of the apparent contradictions in Yeats's theory
arise out of his special nomenclature, in which he makes
not always express distinctions between individuality,
character, and personality. Later, in *A Vision,* he made
the distinctions explicit:

> By being is understood that which divides into Four Faculties,
> by individuality the Will analysed in relation to itself, by per-
> sonality the Will analysed in relation to the free Mask, by char-
> acter Will analysed in relation to the enforced Mask.[63]

Personality is strongest when the being is living in a
condition of greatest beauty and unity of being, while
individuality is strongest when the being is living
through a phase of conflict and fragmentation. Personality is a much freer condition and a more accurate one,
closer to the truth, and distinct from both character and
individuality because closer to unity with the design of
the universe. Personality might be called the fated or
assigned role of the being, character the socially imposed, individuality a product of refusal of both social
and universal role, egotism, false self-assertion, denial.
Personality is religious, character social, individuality
anarchic. The "personal" in such a psychology is not
antithetical to the universal, though the "individual"—
or "individuated"—is antipathetic to the timeless and
spaceless community of spirits that is reality. Personality flourishes in a harmonious world that emulates the
universal order, and such a condition leads men to what
Yeats would later describe as the Brahmanical self. The

daimon or genius or potential reality of the man makes eternal reality *actuel,* contemporaneous with the separated being of the man. Hence the "self" whose expression is of such importance to Yeats is not the individual being with his specialized greedy desire to perpetuate and extend his existence but the immortal element worthy of entry into the community of spirit.

The deeper forms of self-expression were modes of transcending the daily self. Hence Yeats's early acceptance of the idea of self-expression could be integrated with the transcendental ideals that came to him both through the literature of the nineteenth century and through his own explorations of the subterranean tradition of the occult. And, in the intensive studies that occupied his mind from about 1912 to 1924, he could sharpen and trim and clarify his ideas through prolonged immersion in European philosophy and fresh incursions into Buddhist and Hindu thought in the newly available works of such Oriental philosophers as Suzuki. The elaborations of these ideas in *Per Amica Silentia Lunae* and *A Vision* produced an aesthetic psychology of history, a projection beyond poetics of ideas developed in the process of defining the poet's nature and possibilities. From those two books emerged certain ideas, notably those of Mask and Image, that are qualifications of the distinctions so far discussed; but the fundamental poetics remained constant.[64]

Implied in Yeats's poetic dramaturgy are several categories of poetic expression, overlapping and at times contradictory. The following definitions are, as will be clear, not neatly demarcated one from another. They serve as provisional modes of establishing the several dramatic qualities that, in sum, shape the consequences in poetic practice of Yeats's long meditation on person and poem, man and work.

Five Modes, One Poet

In the categories of Yeats's theory and practice, the poet speaks in any of five separable functions:

1. He may speak as the individuated being whose life gives weight to his words, recalling in this action the sentimental verses of the returning Irish exile. He is then preoccupied with discovering the language that will contain the "actual thoughts of a man at a passionate moment of life. . . ."[65] The "interesting life" of the man, his sincerity in self-revelation, and his engagement in important public affairs—these are the implied criteria of such poems as "The Municipal Gallery Revisited":

> You that would judge me, do not judge alone
> This book or that, come to this hallowed place
> Where my friends' portraits hang and look thereon;
> Ireland's history in their lineaments trace;
> Think where man's glory most begins and ends,
> And say my glory was I had such friends.[66]

And this attitude toward the relation between poet and poem is present in such conscience-searching as

> Did that play of mine send out
> Certain men the English shot? [67]

The poems are not always free of self-indulgence and an emotional claim that requires responses in excess of the realized substance of the poetry. "The Municipal

Gallery Revisited" seems to me such a poem, the claim for the Mancini portrait of Lady Gregory being a prime example, and the general bravado embarrassing. The audience is asked to accept estimates that are false and look on at pieties that are largely pose:

> Heart-smitten with emotion I sink down,
> My heart recovering with covered eyes . . .

followed two stanzas later by

> My mediaeval knees lack health until they bend . . .

In the midst of a poem convoking the images of thirty years, this posturing is the very sort of egotism that, he had noted in his journal, came from characterization in self-utterance. For we are here recalled to Yeats's personal interests, his involvement in the concept of hierarchy. It actually serves no function in the poem, is indeed clearly out of place in the syntax of the stanza. We are asked to indulge Yeats as he indulged himself.

"The Municipal Gallery Revisited" shows the dangers of this mode, his attempt to present himself as participant in a historical drama, with the persuasion that his importance outside the poem would validate otherwise invalid claims. The poem is parasitic on his other accomplishments. It is "given weight" not by his life outside the poem but, so far as an audience is concerned, by its reference to some other verbal structure. To turn to the other poem cited above, "The Man and the Echo" (see n. 67), the lines about *Cathleen ni Houlihan* refer to a previous verbal structure in one sense, in another to the remorse of conscience that is the poem's main line of interest:

> Did that play of mine send out
> Certain men the English shot?
> Did words of mine put too great strain
> On that woman's reeling brain?
> Could my spoken words have checked
> That whereby a house lay wrecked?
> And all seems evil until I
> Sleepless would lie down and die.[68]

The urgency of the personal reference is accentuated by the poet's attempt to see his experience as a general category, as if it were not his but an objective form. In this context, the imperfectly rhymed utterance comes as a shock, a terrible revelation of responsibility. It is hardly necessary to know the play, less necessary to know its great impact on its audience. We are asked to accept it as one more burden on the conscience of the speaker, and the speaker is a man facing the weight of his experience before death. The special Irish historical reference is seen as part of a world in which the webs of consequence tremble at each human action.

The temptation of this mode is that in reminiscence and self-assertion the poet will force a sentimental claim, allowing the habitual associations of the verse to carry a burden excessive to the occasion. For it to succeed, the poet has to look on his persona in the poetry as an invention operating according to the laws of his poetic dramaturgy. The love poems to Maud Gonne are a case in point, their chief distinction coming from the poet's capacity to objectify his passionate involvement with this other person and to elaborate her identity, shape her to a symbolic form. Thus the individuated being is shaped into a poetic figure, its validity not to be tested by the poet's sincerity (the equality between experience and art) in the biographical sense, but in the delicacy and strength of the context created by successive works of art.

In this instance, the words are "given weight" by a previous verbal structure, but that structure is the body of the poetry. The poems in *The Wild Swans at Coole* which compose, in effect, a farewell to Maud Gonne would be unbearable in their self-abasement and passive adoration if they were not seen as modulations of an obsessive design, fulfillments and negations, dead ends to a barren passion.[69] They are ungrudging acts of generosity that form necessary elements in a design that has to be brought to term and fullness. So the unimproving spectacle of a suave and utterly controlled technique in the service of an adolescent passion becomes a dramatic force, a part of a prototypical human history.

Thus the individuated man in his web of old associations and attachments, whether those are local or political or sexual, expresses through his life a poetic value. But this can be supported only if the life is seen as a construction, the life being an artifact, the poem a linguistic analogue to the deliberately shaped form of experience. Nature becomes intelligible by an imaginative act that discerns in experience the implied construction. The man in the poem is a specialized form of the man in life, a phantasmagoria. But the dramatic reference of the language is to the process from which the phantasmagoria is liberated, and when the inventive attention lapses we get such lines as "My mediaeval knees lack health until they bend" intervening in a structure to which they have only accidental relevance. Or we get such doting poems as "His Phoenix" or "Broken Dreams," surfaces of self-deceptive rhetoric smoothly denying the abyss of sentimentality that they have in fact opened.

The justification of such lapses is, as already noted, the weight given by a previous verbal structure, but beyond this a sense of life as a symbolic complex motivates the poetics. Yeats saw his most deeply affiliated friends and enemies as part of his spiritual "coven," a congress of beings that were the inscrutable dream of his fated genius: in the terms of *A Vision,* his Body of Fate was the dream of his Daimon.[70] And that Daimon was the ultimate self to which he was indissolubly wed. He came to control and comprehend his life insofar as he understood his Daimon's dream, and in his poems he came as close as any man could to that comprehension.

The individual man, then, in this aspect, is close to the poetic figure of naïve romanticism that Yeats at one point in his life accepted as the prototypical poetic figure:

> We should write out our own thoughts in as nearly as possible the language we thought them in, as though in a letter to an intimate friend. We should not disguise them in any way; for our lives give them force as the lives of people in plays give force to their words.[71]

In practice, he infrequently relied on this concept of the poem as pure "letter to the world"; but he did conceive of his poetry as a drama in which he as individual man had a role, as a play in which a given utterance would gain force by relation to a previous one. So his private life became public matter.

2. The dividing line between private individual and social character is thin enough, but there is an aspect of Yeats in which he takes himself as a social character, as representative of his class, station, and culture. Typically in his poems, he then portrays himself as a being caught between his social identity (character) and his permanent soul (personality), which grants him entry into a spiritual community.

Many of Yeats's most famous and accomplished poems treat this situation, the "Dialogue of Self and Soul" most clearly, "Vacillation" most fully, "Meditations in Time of Civil War" at greatest length, "Nineteen Hundred and Nineteen" perhaps most ambitiously.

In "Nineteen Hundred and Nineteen" he takes the position of spokesman for his civilization as its deluded pursuit of the idea of progress without evil breaks down under the pressures of the Great War. His concerns in this poem are not those of personal associations, old friends, except inferentially, so that he is representative of general historical patterns, and by intent. In this and other poems written in the same mode, it is often difficult to distinguish between symptom and symbol, the personal illness being predicated as widely applicable. An historical phase perfects certain possibilities—for good or evil—in men and shapes the outlines of the human mind with compelling clarity. In "Nineteen Hundred and Nineteen" he adopts the editorial "we" with the motive of appealing to the experience of his contemporaries who have suffered the same historical set of events:

> We too had many pretty toys when young:
> A law indifferent to blame or praise,
> To bribe or threat . . .
> Public opinion ripening for so long
> We thought it would outlive all future days.
> O what fine thought we had because we thought
> That the worst rogues and rascals had died out.[72]

The poet is here participating in the universal delusion that history could be purified of evil, and in the shattering of that notion:

> . . . a drunken soldiery
> Can leave the mother, murdered at her door,
> To crawl in her own blood, and go scot-free;
> The night can sweat with terror as before
> We pieced our thoughts into philosophy,
> And planned to bring the world under a rule,
> Who are but weasels fighting in a hole.[73]

But this measured self-reproach is an attempt to speak of the permanent human capacity for blinding itself to its own malice and an articulation of the poor best that "we" all thought and felt in that distant world before the terrible massive wars: it is ironically offered and measured by an almost proudly gleeful knowledge of evil.

It expresses the temporal community of spirit in history, measured by a knowledge of the community of extrahistoric spirit. This overriding spirit is malicious and sadistic, revealed in a diabolic burst of energy emergent from whirling dust. In Yeats's "Thoughts upon the Present State of the World" (the original title of "Nineteen Hundred and Nineteen"),[74] the sadistic spirit of the world is never remote, so that the poem seems as much a reaction against social realities as an expression of religious ones. The "unpleasantness," the surrendering shudder before unruly malice, comes from the perversity of superior knowledge. The knowledge of evil in this poem is so dominant that it suggests that only evil is permanent, real, valid.

I choose "Nineteen Hundred and Nineteen" because it is a poem in which Yeats sees his own experience at a level of abstraction deliberately rarer than that of his poems oriented toward specifically Irish history. The poem was occasioned by the disorders of war in Ireland during the terror of the Black and Tans, which became a world-wide struggle as he contemplated the state of the civilization of Europe. Ordinarily in Yeats the conflict is not seen as an occasion for this peculiar blending of historicism with personal assertion and prophetic revelation, nor does he so baldly identify himself with the best thinkers and speakers of his day, even ironically.

More typically the conflict between social identity and permanent reality is the source from which the poetic instance emerges. The socially and biologically limited being is juxtaposed with the supernatural and even superhuman element, is shaken and qualified by that element. The condition of being here "treated" is that of the sickened and divided self that Yeats saw in the miseries of the friends of his youth. In the "Dialogue of Self and Soul," he attempts to cast out the remorse attendant on such division and so attain the integrated (and simplified) condition of a natural identity. He moves in such poems from a condition of self-pity and

moral paralysis to the acceptance of role figured in the
inspired speech of "Tom the Lunatic":

> 'Whatever stands in field or flood,
> Bird, beast, fish or man,
> Mare or stallion, cock or hen,
> Stands in God's unchanging eye
> In all the vigour of its blood;
> In that faith I live or die.' [75]

In the manuscript, the last line reads, " 'In that faith I
live *and* die,' " and it was such an unaltering faith in
the perpetuity of just passion toward which he moved
in the poems predicated on a divided state of being.

And his very attitude toward that state fluctuated,
so that in "Vacillation" he oscillated between options
only to accept ultimately the human limits that make
conflict the law of our condition. Because of his sense
of the reality of biological and social limit as well as the
claims of the super human, he could order a range of
experience that would include the reminiscent personal
and move out to the historical or biological limits of
men and from there to a final religious vision. The
paradigm of this mode is "Among School Children,"
beginning as a lament on the defeat of human expectations and, in its first version, ending coolly with the observation that the world of permanent forms mocks
every great man and his enterprise, but in its final version tearing the fabric of its vision to permit the emergence of the symbolic tree. [76]

In many ways the poems that incorporate so wide
and objective a range of matters are the poems and accomplishments that we think of as Yeats. The weakness
of the procedure is that in this sense of poetry the

"poem" becomes a step toward a condition in which the contemplative act is possible; the poem is healing, therapeutic. It brings its writer and reader smoothly to the ultimate, and there it stops, with the implied proviso that beyond this point language is useless. Yeats's multiple commitments, to his individuality (his despised "originality," his equally despised "point of view," his style), to his character (his Irishness, his sense of social responsibility, his representative historical being), to his personality or timeless role—the tension of these commitments becomes a species of historical and personal drama, short of what he took to be the true poetic. The exaltation posited by the poem's conclusion can then be called into question: If this is the poem's substance, why is it not the very texture of the whole? Even in so great a poem as "Among School Children," with its sophisticated surface of benign retrospect, the interplay of naturalistic and symbolic tone, the complaint against old age, the sudden unforgettable apostrophe to the chestnut tree—we can still ask why the moment of enraptured apprehension of reality should be so brief, whether it does genuinely transcend the limits so fully and even affectionately treated in the bulk of the poem. The poem flirts with the danger of casting doubt on its own resolutions, largely because it exhibits in its dramaturgy a multiple poetics.

These doubts are very real, and they are part of the immediate texture of this and other poems. It does not seem to me to diminish their impact or value in any way, but it does help to place them in the intentions of Yeats's poetics. One way of phrasing the intention is to assume that he is examining the emergence of reality in a multiplicity of processes, the poem being the instrument of a spiritual quest. These poems, then, are concerned with the conditions of poetic apprehension, and they are in part pre-poetic.

3. Once the poet has, by the act of imagining the process that conditioned the visionary truth, attained the state of receptive poetic grace, he can then speak as prophet and pure agent of the community of spirit. In this guise the poet is embodiment and voice of a passionate revelation of structures beyond his comprehension when acting as social or historical being. It is this sudden emergence, with the rational connective shattered, that distinguishes the concluding outburst of "Among School Children," and it is this revelation with which the insistently balanced structures of "Byzantium" attempt to cope. The swan of "Leda and the Swan" is a pure example, as is the rough beast of "The Second Coming." But it is not merely in prophecy of the *Anima Mundi* in its historical connections that such poetic insight is granted, for it appears also in "Her Vision in a Wood" and such poems as "Her Anxiety," lyrics speaking from his grasp of dramatic and lyric matter embedded deeply in simple human need.

The moment of insight emerges from a process of struggle. It seldom appears purely because, as Yeats said in his journal, "The one reason for putting our actual situation into our art is that the struggle for complete affirmation may be, often must be, that art's chief poignancy." [77] But once the struggle had come to resolution, the art could make its affirmation of identity with the timeless spirit of the world. The poems in this category are frequently related to some prior verbal

structure because they require some substratum of
process if they are to emerge. "Byzantium," for instance, is not only the expression of a lifetime of meditation on the concept of image, man, shade (each an
aspect of the human being, the image *not* being the
term used in literary vocabulary), but it is an extension
beyond the ground cleared by "Sailing to Byzantium,"
taking up an essential ambiguity characteristically revealed in the earlier poem with its play upon conflict
between biological and spiritual reality. The "Two
Songs from a Play" could as well be titled "Two Songs
Based on a Play," for the discursive matter of *Resurrection,* both that in the final version and the matter of the
more discursive manuscript and earlier versions, was
their foundation. Based on that matter he was elevated
to a point where he could apprehend in synoptic form
the vista on which the play at its close merely opened.

The "previous verbal structure" was necessary for
him, as writer, and in one sense a major result of his
dramaturgy is to compel his audience to identity with
the poet as poetic being moving through the process of
experience. There is no point in my attempting to legis-
late against a habit of commentary so deeply ingrained
in criticism of Yeats as that—largely initiated by
Cleanth Brooks's pioneer essay [78]—of referring all obscurities in the poems to (often more obscure) passages
in Yeats's prose. But generally speaking, the poems
themselves are more relevant than the prose, and the
manuscripts are frequently much more relevant than
adjacent poems. When there is a lapse in syntax or unclarity in symbol or image, the "previous verbal structure" referred to is often an earlier draft of the poem.

Perhaps the most egregious example is the title of "Sailing to Byzantium": in the finished poem the protagonist is already in Byzantium, and the title vestigially refers to an earlier version in which it took the poet approximately two weeks to make the journey.[79] The chief point is that the poems of pure revelation—what Yeats himself would have considered pure poetry—are possible only within the impure context of the life of the divided self struggling through successive nightmares of deceptive lures.

4. The poet may speak as overt dramatist. In this role he is maker of dramatis personae, the shaper of personifications of passions, whether in stage plays or nominal lyrics. Even the poems of self-utterance, as suggested above, must to be successful attain the status of objectified drama. In these works the poet comes as close as ever he can to autonomy, for he is not suffering the mediumship of passive agency nor is he committed to his own "character" even as device. He is not treating merely himself as persona but treating personae as expressions of his will, and in his will is their fulfillment. He is then most godly, freely shaping and casting. He rests in his identification with the great dramatist of the universe. Yeats's plays are the exemplars of his action in this mode, and their attempt to approximate what he called the great ritual of nature shows his careful attention to the voice of established norms—Christ, Oedipus, Cuchulain, Queen, beggar, stroller, old man, and boy—which he brings to perfection.

In the lyric poems, too, he shapes personae, not only out of his own being but out of admired historical figures like Swift or invented figures like Crazy Jane

(Cracked Mary) [80] or the man and woman young and old. These personae, like those of his plays or those wrested from his individual fate, are "voices," personifications and passionate embodiments that evoke Yeats's partisanship, his conviction of their importance and ultimate propriety, their decorum in the universal structure. It is in his loyalty to these figures, his conviction of their rightness, that his employment of the persona differs from that of Pound and Eliot.[81] Pound's use of Malatesta is baffling in its ambiguities, and in some sense he seems to feel that Malatesta's complete wrongness is more admirable than any possible rightness, while at the same time he disclaims identity of himself with Siggy. Eliot's use of Gerontion and Prufrock as personae is motivated chiefly by his abiding contempt for their human incompetence. But Yeats's personae are the affirmations won by his struggle, so that the only persona regarded with amusement or with dislike in his poems is usually some abstraction from his own being. Crazy Jane and Tom the Lunatic he accepts and admires.

5. The poet makes a statement when he acts as editor, maker of books. He shapes a poetic construct even when he is editing, say, *The Oxford Book of Modern Verse*, and the statement made by Yeats in selecting for that anthology was a definition of a poetics. But more crucially, especially with a poet operating in a multiple poetics, his editing of his own work, selection, arrangement, rewriting, is a creative and shaping act. After the emergence of the individual constructs, the poems, he is faced with the problem of shaping the structure of a book. The most notable instance in Yeats's work is

his preparation of the text of *The Tower*, his resurrection of an earlier poem, his exclusion of several poems (notably the sequence "A Woman Young and Old") written well before the book was to go to press. The solidity of *The Tower* has often been noted, and the reading of individual poems in it is frequently altered by their relation to the remainder of the book.[82]

In this respect "Sailing to Byzantium" is revealing, for if the poem resolves the problem of old age and art, there is something rather odd in Yeats's following it with a poem ("The Tower") which offers a significantly different treatment of the subject and a continued examination of images dominant in "Sailing to Byzantium." Seen in the context of the book, "Sailing to Byzantium" is a definition or sketch of a problem rather than a denial of it; and the very existence (in a later book) of "Byzantium" illustrates that it did not exhaust the problem in any sense. Yeats was urged toward writing "Byzantium" at least in part to answer a criticism of the ambiguity of the last stanza of "Sailing to Byzantium," Sturge Moore pointing out that the golden bird was as natural an object as any other. He saw that the golden bird was a captive of nature, being compelled to sing of "What is past, or passing, or to come," the syntactic analogue of "Whatever is begotten, born, and dies." Seen in the total structure of the book, the bird's captive state becomes ever more obvious, and Moore in his commentary was writing with awareness of the total web of Yeats's attitudes, obsessions and habits of work.[83]

In Yeats's "construction" of *The Tower*, he was interested in making a design so that he could comprehend what he took to be the major drift of his poetry. With the book in hand, he wrote to Olivia Shakespear that he was astonished at its bitterness,[84] and certainly in the succeeding book (*The Winding Stair*) he made a fierce effort to cast out remorse ("Repentance keeps my heart impure") and affirm passion, so that *The Winding Stair* can very profitably be read as reaction to *The Tower.*

A book of Yeats's could be an extremely careful selection or it might conscientiously take up themes in order to exorcise them. It was always an extremely careful ordering. The result was that his books articulate a body of related data and feelings, taking up a set of mutually illuminating obsessions that were at the center of phases of his being: the elegiac tone of *The Wild Swans at Coole* and the didactic projection beyond that fulfilled tone to the newly emerging preoccupations with sex and history; the sexual and historical concerns of *Michael Robartes and the Dancer;* the testamentary motives of *The Tower;* the attempt to move past remorse to purified passion in *The Winding Stair.*

All these five functions were practiced by Yeats before he entered his later phase, but increasingly they were exercised with deliberate full awareness. The watershed of his life in 1917 is generally associated with his marriage and *A Vision,* and, in addition to those crucially rewarding events, his life from 1917 to 1924 was marked by other summary activities. The writing of his autobiography was one, and the collection of his work for the definitive (to 1922) Macmillan edition was another, for they compelled him to observe the patterns of his life, the forms of his work, and the relation between them. From that point, in effect, he entered a fresh career.

There are in Yeats two complete careers. The first extends from his earliest work to the personalist and elegiac poems of *The Wild Swans at Coole,* which to many readers is the highest achievement of Yeats's poetry. It is certainly the ultimate expression of his early career. If only the poems written up to *The Wild Swans at Coole* were extant, Yeats would seem to be essentially the poet described in my *W. B. Yeats, Self-Critic,* that is, a poet beginning with the basic prescriptions of the 1890's who sought a defined subject matter at once personal and universal—the Irish and the occult—and a style that would be appropriate to that subject matter; who rejected that early style after his experience in the theater and turned his powers toward adapting his dramatic manner to suit lyric needs; and who then extended the range of his dramatic style to include public and individual experience intimate in tone. The ultimate middle style is most evident in his great elegy "In Memory of Major Robert Gregory," in which he exhibited his mastery over his freshly developed idiom and achieved understanding control over the dominant figures of his early imagination. This poem stands at a point of balance between the maturing force of his work from 1910 to 1917 and the complete release of his powers that came with his later poetry.

The second career begins with an act of purification, the *Autobiography,* in which he defined the poet's nature, and an act of elaboration in which he adapted to his sense of experience the totality of history. *A Vision* is essentially a psychology of history rather than a philosophy, and it served a double function, that of telling Yeats where he was at his given moment in the history of the human mind and that of providing a base for his poetic vision. From the security granted by that underpinning, he could speak not as an individuality, not out of his social character, but out of his identification with and knowledge of objective reality.

I use the term "objective" deliberately because the difference between the early and later career seems to me to reside particularly in his later capacity for looking on his knowledge and experience as *not* his own. He came to separate other from self to the extent that he could separate character from personality. The change is not a mere shift in quality of affection, from tenderness to rage, for instance, nor is it a shift from personal to mythical, from Irish to world-wide. It is a change in the *sense* of material, not just its feeling for him but its actual reference. If we take as examples two poems that strike closest to his personal obsessions, that is, two that come out of his relation to Maud Gonne, the matter may be clarified.

In "Presences," which is the last of the farewell series to Maud Gonne in *The Wild Swans at Coole*, he deliberately imagines a remembered scene that will allow him one hyperbolic statement on his love:

> This night has been so strange that it seemed
> As if the hair stood up on my head.
> From going-down of the sun I have dreamed
> That women laughing, or timid or wild,

In rustle of lace or silken stuff,
Climbed up my creaking stair. They had read
All I had rhymed of that monstrous thing
Returned and yet unrequited love.
They stood in the door and stood between
My great wood lectern and the fire
Till I could hear their hearts beating:
One is a harlot, and one a child
That never looked upon man with desire,
And one, it may be, a queen.[85]

The opening two lines set the anecdotal frame: The most extraordinary thing happened to me. To which we are supposed to reply, "Really?" Yes: you see . . . And so on. The deliberate shape of the poem is that of ironic self-protection: You won't believe this, but. . . . And the entire poem is phrased in so arch and tiptoe a style as to suggest a man who is conducting a very apologetic nonsensical enterprise. At the close, we are supposed to say, "I see. Someone you think highly of." For the qualifications tell us that we are not to take seriously the literal statements; it seemed as if; it was so real that I could (you will never believe this) hear their hearts beating; "And one, it may be, a queen." In other words, don't think that *I* don't see through all this nonsense, but in the poetry game, you know, a man has to use a few stretchers.

It is a compliment, prettily turned in a courtly way, and the tone of the last line suggests its motive: I've brought together the items in this pretty fancy, the range of feminine experience, the invented dream, merely to praise one woman; here it is, an offering. There is nothing exceptionable in this display of sentiment.

It is, in short, elegant trifling handled with sweet rhetorical grace. In this poem of sentiment, the figures of queen, harlot, and child are mechanisms that trigger a response to an aging man with misted eyes in his anecdotage. Take it for what it is, it is not much, nor does it help matters to associate it with Iseult and Maud Gonne. It is really associated—poetically—with the persona of Yeats as aging frustrated lover engaged in an act of generous selfless forgiveness. And the "queen" is the woman of that persona. In the poem this is transparent, as it is in the other poems of the sequence, all very low-keyed, modest in assertion, claiming sentiment as their province, anecdote as their mode of discourse.

I am not questioning the "success" of the poem, and I am not even questioning the validity of the genre. But the sense of the poem is predicated on a sense of the experience, the overt possibility that the speaker and the poet are one, and the aim is to project a persona that will not discredit the poet as individual human being but will show his biological good sense. The poem has an eye to its effect on his reputation as a social creature.

In Yeats's own terms, these motives are poetically secondary, and he came to accept with some cheerfulness that the persona projected in his poetry had nothing to do with his daily being, was in many ways its antithesis. The care for "characterization" that he came to think of as "egotism" was, as the comments above on "The Municipal Gallery Revisited" show, never completely obliterated from his work. Once liberated from the necessity of being attractive, he could express his total apprehension more readily. He had to take less seriously the possible judgment of others and more seriously his destined role. The "unpleasantness" of his later work and its insistence on certain terrible moments are a product of his dissociation of his social character from his poetic personality.

An example of his willingness to explore the unpleasant is "Her Vision in the Wood," which is not only one of his best poems but an historical ending to the romantic obsession with the figure of the *femme fatale*.[86] Here the figure of the woman is aged and incapable of exciting the passion of men, having lost the beauty for which "Troy passed away in one high funeral gleam, / And Usna's children died." The woman had been in his imagination from his first reading of Swinburne's *Chastelard*, and it was this obsessive figure of the romantic imagination that had most deeply affected his sense of femininity and even perhaps preconditioned him to his passive and self-destructive role *vis à vis* Maud Gonne. Richard Ellmann reads the poem as a portrayal of the Adonis legend, as in part it is, but it is so "remarkable" because the legend is used as a device for purifying Yeats's imagination of received associations and habitual sentiment.[87] It is a very peculiar Venus, in her old age and knowledgeable in the painting of the Quattrocento, that appears in the poem:

> Dry timber under that rich foliage,
> At wine-dark midnight in the sacred wood,
> Too old for a man's love I stood in rage
> Imagining men. Imagining that I could
> A greater with a lesser pang assuage
> Or but to find if withered vein ran blood,

> I tore my body that its wine might cover
> Whatever could recall the lip of lover.

Her lacerations are turned against herself, so that the "Dolores" of the romantic agony becomes, in a rage of frustration, her own victim:

> And after that I held my fingers up,
> Stared at the wine-dark nail, or dark that ran
> Down every withered finger from the top;
> But the dark changed to red, and torches shone,
> And deafening music shook the leaves; a troop
> Shouldered a litter with a wounded man,
> Or smote upon the string and to the sound
> Sang of the beast that gave the fatal wound.

Envious of the procession of apparent immortals, she finds herself caught up in their passionate grief and joins their lament:

> All stately women moving to a song
> With loosened hair or foreheads grief-distraught,
> It seemed a Quattrocento painter's throng,
> A thoughtless image of Mantegna's thought—
> Why should they think that are for ever young?
> Till suddenly in grief's contagion caught,
> I stared upon his blood-bedabbled breast
> And sang my malediction with the rest.

Finally she recognizes that she is at once victim and torturer, Venus, boar, and Adonis:

> That thing all blood and mire, that beast-torn wreck,
> Half turned and fixed a glazing eye on mine,
> And, though love's bitter-sweet had all come back,
> Those bodies from a picture or a coin
> Nor saw my body fall nor heard it shriek,
> Nor knew, drunken with singing as with wine,

That they had brought no fabulous symbol there
But my heart's victim and its torturer.[88]

We are a long way from the mere desire to praise a particular woman and very close to the satisfaction of the persona of the woman eager for her own praise and indifferent to her adoring lover. Here *La Belle Dame sans Merci* is given her quietus.

This poem is of a different genre from "Presences," and here one can see how differently the prototypical figures of the imagination are handled. For the child, harlot, and queen of "Presences" were not to be taken literally, were overtly presented as anecdotal equivalents for a personal feeling. Here the fabulous figures of the woman's dream *are* to be taken literally, as is the figure of her heart's victim and torturer, and we are to assume that *these* presences are something more than metaphor to enrich the feelings of a cultivated sensibility. They are instead entries into the permanent forms of the human imagination, not by their echo of Frazer, the citation of Mantegna, the realization of possibilities of Swinburne, though those cultural forces are part of the predication, but through the full articulation, the urgent voice of the speaker.

The poem is one of a sequence of poems, "A Woman Young and Old," which begins with a poem coming straight out of the domestic experience of the Yeats family. In March of 1926, Yeats recorded the following diary entry:

George has just told me that yesterday she said to Anne "I don't like so and so," so and so being a little boy of Anne's age, "He is a very nasty child." Anne replied "Yes but he has such lovely hair and his eyes are as cold as a March wind." I should put that into verse for it is the cry of every woman who loves a blackguard.

The anecdote went rapidly into verse:

    a. It is but waste of breath to say
    b. She hears me strike the board and say
        That she is under ban
        To all good men and women,
        Being mentioned with a man
        That has the worst of all bad names
    a. If thereon she replies
    b. And thereupon replies
        That his hair is beautiful
    a. And cold as the March wind his eyes
    b. Cold as the March wind his eyes [89]

Its first version is a simple general, rather wearied statement with an if . . . then predication, which in the second version shifts to the perceiving point of view of "she," as if Yeats had immediately, after his first idle notation of the idea, seen a perspective from which the statement could become dramatic, that is, the emergent structure of "A Woman Young and Old." The voice might be that of an anxious and overwrought father, but the substance is ". . . the cry of every woman who loves a blackguard." The material was distanced by his poetic grasp of the particular, so that his seven-year-old daughter's precocious ability to distinguish aesthetic from ethical quality is not taken for the piece of extraordinary childish wit that in fact it was. And the actually amazed father is transformed to the persona of the outraged speaker.

    I take these two poems as extremes of origin, the one emerging directly from an amused and perceptive family life, the other from the depths of the romantic consciousness, and the two brought together through the poet acting in his editorial capacity as shaper of constructs from constructs. In these two poems an objective readiness to play with his experience and to shape it in conformity with an external ideal manifests itself, so that he looks on his own experience and his imagination of mythical figures as equally data, manna, for which he deserves no personal credit and for which he need take no personal blame. There is a casual, almost professional, ease and bravura. What keeps it from frivolity and irresponsibility is his acceptance of the poetic roles and subjects as his given burden. He stands behind these figures, and in effect stands behind himself. There is no evasion.

Even in his most designedly impersonal poems he conveys the impression of engaged sensibility. For all the multiplicity of surface, the singleness of his poems, their mark of a master hand, is always evident, as if his intimacy increased with his detachment and his capacity for yielding himself grew with his indifference to his role as social being. The result is not at all like the intimate impersonal meditations of Wallace Stevens, nor is his being replaced by objects or by processes of language, as the Imagists and their varied descendants so wonderfully managed. Nor does he justify the solipsistic world that Suzanne Langer attempts to claim as the artist's special realm. His presence is not that of a sensibility only but of an intervening human force, essentially unrefined, and indifferent to our presence. He is not asking for credit; he is simply there, inescapable. Hence there is a sense in which his work, so monumental and so polished, continuously shatters its own illusions. The poetry to about 1915 seems to be striving toward accomplishment and recognition, asking us to observe what the poet has done, but from 1917 on there is in the poetry the passionate coldness, the neglect of self, that he ascribed to Shakespeare's heroes and heroines. His attainments then grew out of a form of surrender in which he abdicated his claim to consideration. He did not care about our judgment; he suffered it without reckoning. He acted his role, and social or aesthetic criteria had no relevance. The several shibboleths of critical theory became meaningless:

Talk to me of originality and I will turn on you with rage. I am a crowd, I am a lonely man, I am nothing. . . . The heroes of Shakespeare convey to us through their looks, or through the metaphorical patterns of their speech, the sudden enlargement of their vision, their ecstacy at the approach of death . . . but all must be cold; no actress has ever sobbed when she played Cleopatra, even the shallow brain of a producer has never thought of such a thing. The supernatural is present, cold winds blow across our hands, upon our faces, the thermometer falls, and because of that cold we are hated by journalists and groundlings. There may be in this or that detail painful tragedy, but in the whole work none . . . nor is it any different with lyrics, songs, narrative poems. . . .[90]

If he were to be worthy of a prominent part in the play, he could not break up his lines to weep. His role as lyric poet compelled him to a variety of modes, which he accepted without care for misunderstanding. The painfulness or unpleasantness of any given moment would be measured and placed in the total perspective of the work. Bravado and negligence and even self-indulgence might be justified by their relation to a large symbolic drama.

Ultimately, Yeats came to look on his poetic role as a form of mediumship. To return to the arguments of Eliot and Pound discussed in the first section of this chapter, his poetics is not radically divergent from the concept of poet as agent and maker that Eliot so cogently phrased in his early essays. Playing on the ambiguities of the term, one might say that one medium of poetry was the personae, the symbolic dramatic figures, granted to Yeats through experience and study, and that he had to be faithful to what they permitted. Yet he was not passive and helpless before them; he was a conscious, desirous shaper and not merely inert. He had to purify the personal of the accidental and could do so only by accepting traditional prosodic forms and symbols widely distributed and of some longevity.

Hence in form and subject he thought of himself as a deeply traditional poet. He wrote in 1936 that ". . . those themes we share and inherit so long as they engage our emotions come first." And what engaged the emotions was not very remote from the "wonderful, sad, happy people moving through the scenery of my dreams" that were evoked for him by Pre-Raphaelite painting and which he so missed in art of the modernist movement. The surrender before the medium that is a central thread in modernist art criticism he saw as a surrender to fate, an abdication of the artist's proper role:

I thought when I was young—Walt Whitman had something to do with it—that the poet, painter and musician should do nothing but express themselves. When the laboratories, pulpits, and newspapers had imposed themselves in the place of tradition the thought was our protection. It may be so still in the provinces, but sometimes when the provinces are out of earshot I may speak the truth. A poet is justified not by the expression of himself, but by the public he finds or creates; a public made by others to his hand if he is a mere popular poet, but a new public, a new form of life, if he is a man of genius.

I say against all the faggots that it is our first business to paint, or describe, desirable people, places, states of mind. Rimbaud showed in a famous poem that the picking of lice was a good lawful theme for the Silver Age; the radical critics encourage our painters to decorate the wall with those cubes, triangles, ovoids, that are all stiff under the touch, or with gods and goddesses, distorted by Rubensesque exaggeration, dulled by hard doll-like faces that they may chill desire. We have arrived at that point where in every civilisation Caesar is killed, Alexander catches some complaint and dies; personality is exhausted, that conscious, desirous, shaping fate rules.[91]

The "coldness" that he found desirable was a coldness shaped in heat and passion. This "making" led not to self-expression and the articulation of accidents but to self-discovery and the establishment of norms of being that took their dignified place in the great drama of the universe. Poetry of this sort was not the higher algebra of metaphor, a species of play written out of indifference to his audience but an attempt to transform the conditions of human being by reminding the audience of its potentialities.

The concept of personality that emerges from the scrutiny of Yeats's theory and practice is inclusive and tough. It is also very risky, and it reveals an aspect of Yeats that can be too easily overlooked, that is, his capacity for the major effort and major dangers. He

began with a formula that could have led him to grave
sentimental errors, and he so altered the formula in his
lifelong study that he shaped a body of poetry that
creates its own criteria and provides norms that are
challenging and demanding. He carried the ideas of
the Romantic movement to their full fruition, and he
assimilated and qualified the ideas of the modernist
aesthetic. He lived through two major literary periods,
affirming continuities and accepting changes with a
clear sense of tradition rather than convention, and
innovation rather than novelty. His poetry thus represents the widest range of dramatic possibilities, in practice and in implied theory, so that all the major issues
are raised by him. The result, as the late Donald Stauffer observed, was a body of poetry that has the resonance normally found in extended works of literary art,
a corpus of plays, an epic, a novel of large scope.

The grand architecture of his work grows from his
dramatic sense, and this sense in turn is affected by the
processes of his career. At the most simple level, a
great part of the dramatic quality of Yeats comes from
his steady—though occasionally interrupted—development, the happy movement through conflict and failure
to moments of ecstatic revelation, and the purification
and improvement of his control over idiom and subject.
His work is stirring in large part because it is the painstaking record of a success story, of the poet who started
with no more promise than a dozen of his contemporaries but with hard work and good luck became the
one member of the Rhymers' Club whose poetry is
still read for more than historical interest. The career,

even as modified by his rewriting of early poems, is
evident in the *Collected Poems* as an aesthetic drama,
and part of its effectiveness as a dramatic construct
comes from its failures as well as its triumphs. Yeats
created a structure in which the interest and relevance
of any part is crucial but in which not all parts are
equal in intensity or achievement.

A great amount of the best modern poetry is "about"
the poetic enterprise, seen as emblematic of the problems that men face in a disordered world. In this poetry,
the poet is involved in a continual struggle to attain
meaning by contemplation and invention. He makes up
value as he goes along, and the process is close to that
of the jazz musician or the Action painter. The process
of employing all the devices of craft in order to discover significant experience becomes a prime part of
the texture of the work. Nothing is then left out, and
the audience is compelled to undergo the experience
that the artist suffered, is asked to endure with the
artist the pain and wonder of creation. At its worst, this
convention lapses into the cant of "creativity" and the
cult of planned spontaneity. With Yeats this enterprise
is conditioned by the traditions of poetry and by his
clear sense of dramatic function. The totality of his
work provides a context, even a lexicon, in which the
emergent quality of his great poems is more clear, evident, and imposing. The bulk of his work is a necessary
substratum, frequently interesting in itself but mainly
important because it provides structure and context.
Even the lyrics that are not primary accomplishments
benefit from their association with each other and with

the larger symbolic drama of his work. If Yeats is "uneven" he is uneven in the sense that the Sierra Nevada is uneven, and small mountains are mountains.

The unevenness of his poetry is relative. He does not have the long dull stretches of Wordsworth, for instance, and he does not repeat himself in the plodding manner of Hardy. What unevenness Yeats shows comes from the variety of the dramatic enterprise that he undertook as his. Beyond this dramatic variety, his verse is further complicated by his extremely complex sense of iconography and his flexible prosody. He constructed his poetics through constant study, through the most painstaking rewriting of draft, fair copy, and printed poem. He contemplated with full clarity the biographies of his associates in the 1890's for clues that would elucidate his position and restrain him from error. He read widely and deeply in the great poetry of the past, and he carried on a long running argument with his friend Ezra Pound which crystallized his views and spurred him from complacency. The ultimate test was always his own poetry, its references, origins, and processes.

VESTIGES OF CREATION

Whatever I do, poetry will remain a torture.

Gestation

I HAVE already touched briefly upon Yeats's method of composition, but I should like now to consider in detail the origins of two of his most remarkable poems, "After Long Silence" and "Among School Children." We are extremely fortunate in having so complete a record of Yeats's creative processes. Although occasionally vague in the conduct of daily life, he was very orderly in matters having to do with his verse. He kept notebooks from the beginning of his career, and in his journals one can often trace a poem from prose draft to finished, or at least publishable, version. After his marriage, his external life had an increasingly orderly pattern, and from 1917 onward the manuscript collections are comprehensive,

and the manuscript books—always carefully bound—
become even more sumptuous. Many of the poems in
Responsibilities (1914), after initial notation in a white
leather-bound manuscript book, were written on loose
scrappy sheets of paper varying in size and texture;
most of the poems in *The Winding Stair* (1933) began
and frequently fulfilled their form in large bound manuscript books, one in vellum, the others in cardboard
beautifully covered. And Mrs. Yeats saw to it, sometimes by surreptitiously recovering them from waste-
baskets, that the various loose sheets of fair copies and
typescripts were also collected and retained. She could
do nothing about typescripts dispatched to magazine
editors, sometimes with autograph variants, and this in
part accounts for occasional incompleteness of the record.[1]

From this record it is possible to gain an intimate in-
dex to the critical sense that Yeats applied to his work
in the process of composition. Although it is often
baffling to see the sudden leaps and attainments and
lapses of Yeats's imagination, one can see more clearly
the kinds of rational distinctions and choices that he
made. It is only infrequently possible to discern in the
manuscripts how he came to write a certain line, but
his notes and initial drafts and fair copies often exhibit
the temptations and rejections that were his main necessities.

At times the manuscripts help to untangle certain
difficulties in the interpretation of Yeats's poems. The
reading of "After Long Silence" which appears in the
standard textbook *Understanding Poetry* is pretty
clearly shown by the manuscript evidence to be hardly

an accurate reading of the poem.[2] The last line of "Tom the Lunatic," which seems oddly inconclusive in its present form, becomes explicable when seen as a faulty transcription from an admittedly obscure fair copy.[3] And other crucial points in Yeats's verse that have been ignored or skated gently over, such as the Presences of "Among School Children," take on a different aspect.[4] But these illuminations are, from the point of view taken in this chapter, incidental.

I would like to regard this chapter as in part a test of the ideas proposed in the first chapter and as an adumbration of the arguments on iconography and prosody that will appear in chapters iii and iv. And beyond that, the study of variant possibilities in a poem inevitably increases simple appreciation, our pleasure and wonder at the accomplishments of the verse. Yeats's attainments grow in magnitude from scrutiny of his possible failures, and the sense of glory that accompanies great insight eloquently phrased increases with recognition of its difficulty. This has been my chief reward in studying the manuscripts, and it is a reward that I am eager to share.

Louis MacNeice has written of what he calls Yeats's "notorious labor pains" in writing a poem, and Yeats certainly found the writing of poetry a "torture."[5] In fifty years of active work he produced less than four hundred lyric poems that he thought worth preserving as his permanent legacy. Thomas Hardy, in contrast, wrote some nine hundred lyrics in a period of a little over thirty years. Yeats considered a short stanza a good day's work:

Metrical composition is always very difficult to me, nothing is done upon the first day, not one rhyme is in its place; and when at last the rhymes begin to come, the first rough draft of a six-line stanza takes a whole day. At that time [the early '90's] I had not formed a style, and sometimes a six-line stanza would take several days, and not seem finished even then and I had not learnt, as I have now, to put it all out of my head before night, and so the last night was generally sleepless, and the last day a day of nervous strain.[6]

He may have, in his later years, put it all out of his head before night, but when he returned to the manuscripts the following day, the difficulties remained: all those false starts, the lists of rhymes established, tried, and discarded, the stanzas lined out. At times the writing became so illegible that Yeats was forced to consult his wife to decipher a scribble made the preceding day.

Yet his difficulties, marked though they were, were not really extraordinary. There may be "natural" poets who sing as the birds sing, but such poets as Dylan Thomas, John Keats, and Walt Whitman were not among them, nor was Yeats. Yeats was fond of quoting Goethe to the effect that art is art because it is not nature, a commonsensical observation. Poets who have seen the Yeats manuscripts are struck not by their elaborateness or the trouble they exhibit, but by their proximity to their own notebooks and manuscripts. They take heart from seeing that the finished products of Yeats's imagination, so sure and deft and natural in appearance, should have come from ". . . a suffering passion and a labouring thought." [7]

The only word that properly describes the courses which Yeats's poem took from initial impetus to final form is "various." Some poems began with a rather

thorough but synoptic articulation of subject and follow
out the design thus prescribed without major deviation.
His aim in writing such poems seemed to be, quite simply, to find the appropriate atmosphere, iconography,
and dramatic situation that would embody the idea in
the most comprehensive and attractive form. The process is one of embodiment, movement from judgment
and understanding to design and substance (see the
analysis of "After Long Silence" below). Other poems
began not so much with an idea as with a feeling, a
sense of experience and emotion inchoate and immediate, followed by an exploratory effort to secure a body
of felt data that would allow the poem to emerge as an
instrument of understanding and judgment. The term
"objective correlative," which has become, through
Eliot's brilliant essay on "Hamlet and His Problem," a
secure part of our critical vocabulary, is exemplified
clearly in this practice, and perhaps most noticeably in
the letter to Olivia Shakespear that describes the origin
of "Crazy Jane and Jack the Journeyman":

> . . . I went for a walk after dark and there among some great
> trees became absorbed in the most lofty philosophical concep-
> tion I have found while writing *A Vision*. I suddenly seemed to
> understand at last and then I smelt roses. I now realized the na-
> ture of the timeless spirit. Then I began to walk and with my
> excitement came—how shall I say?—that old glow so beautiful
> with its autumnal tint. The longing to touch it was almost un-
> endurable. The next night I was walking in the same path and
> now the two excitements came together. The autumnal image,
> remote, incredibly spiritual, erect, delicate featured, and mixed
> with it the violent physical image, the black mass of Eden.
> Yesterday I put my thoughts into a poem which I enclose, but
> it seems to me a poor shadow of the intensity of the experience.[8]

How very few of these features were brought directly
over into the poem can be seen by referring to its text
(analyzed in chapter iv). The "black mask of Eden"
finds its expression through "Cracked Mary," the violent physical image of Crazy Jane and her terribly remote and intimate Jack the Journeyman. The path
appears in the poem, but the chief similarity in letter
and poem is "intensity," the experience being presented
in a figurative emotional analogue—to return to Eliot's
term, an objective correlative.

"After Long Silence" and "Crazy Jane and Jack the
Jorneyman" represent extremes, and between them
Yeats ran a considerable course. At times neither the
desire to dramatize an idea nor the quest for image and
structure to create an analogue to an intense feeling
was the motivating impulse. Some of the poems begin
with a close contemplation of an icon, followed by an
attempt to examine its various potentialities, so that
"Vacillation," ultimately including an enormous range
of material, began with a simple intensive scrutiny of
the divided tree, and the "Dialogue of Self and Soul"
(originally "Silk, Sword, and Tower," in manuscript)
grew from the physical existence in Yeats's study of a
Samurai sword in a scabbard bound round with stuff
from a Japanese court lady's (*not* Lady Gregory's)
dress.[9] In both instances, the attempt was to find in
these icons—one a subjective symbol, the other an objective image—relations of qualities that would allow
the freest exploration of his own desires and knowledge.

In addition to dramatic, emotional, and iconographic
origins, many of his poems began out of fascination with
simple rhythms of phrase, sentence, or clause that as-

serted a mood, this assertion to be rebuked, recharacterized, or accepted and followed out. After the initial emotion of spirit that moved him toward "Crazy Jane and Jack the Journeyman," he turned over and over in his mind the important phrase, "the door unlatched," until he had effected a rhythmic structure where it could appear with greatest force. So his sense of cadence requiring a search for consenting movements of line and syntax impelled many poems, and many lines within poems. One striking instance of this appears in his use of a phrase from Bergson in "Dialogue of Self and Soul." When Bergson twice described the intellect as dealing with "this and that and the other thing" in an indiscriminate catalogue of abstractions, Yeats underlined the phrase and with the ultimate elision of "t'other" brought it into a crucial place in his poem. In the context of the poem, the phrase magnified and specified meaning, but only this one phrase, as far as I can determine, took pride of place in Yeats's poetry, although his reading of Bergson was methodically thorough and his underlining of sections of *Creative Evolution* was—unlike marginalia in much of his philosophic reading—sympathetic and free of ironic commentary. It was not the idea, much more cogently phrased in many passages of *Creative Evolution*, but the compressed disdain of the rhythm, the tight linear construction of phrase, that arrested his attention and gave him the cue to its usefulness in his own poem.

Yet, in spite of such occasional directness of movement from reading to poem, from idea to artifact, the process indicated by Yeats's drafts was extremely elaborate, and much more often than not the initial impetus or phrasing was left far behind. This is to say that he was not merely annotating or decorating ideas, his own or others', with rhythmic phrases, not merely holding a dead formalized set of judgments up for inspection and uttering solemn injunctions to the uninstructed. Something at once more frivolous and more profound went on as he tested the formalized intention against the requirements of rhyme, syntax, stanza form, and line structure, to say nothing of the arc of experience that the poem invented for itself, its extensive structure commanding changes in intent as much as did the local texture of vowel tone and quantity.

One striking example of the change from initial motive to final form is analyzed below in detail: "Among School Children"; another is "Coole Park, 1929." Before he began work on the latter poem he wrote a prose summary of the projected lyric:

> Describe house in first stanza. Here Synge came, Hugh Lane, Shaw Taylor, many names. I too in my timid youth. Coming and going like migratory birds. Then address the swallows fluttering in their dream like circles. Speak of the rarity of the circumstances that bring together such concords of men. Each man more than himself through whom an unknown life speaks. A circle ever returning into itself.[10]

But when the poem was finished, it did not devote the first stanza to "describing" the house; its speaker merely acts as if he were standing in front of the house and speaks primarily of the works and thoughts that it engendered and protected. He adds only the name of Douglas Hyde to those of Synge, Lane, Taylor, and he so minimizes any reference to his own youth ("There one that ruffled in a manly pose / For all his timid heart . . .") as to make himself anonymous. The idea that the expressive man is spokesman of depths not his, an idea very close to the center of Yeats's thought, is not present overtly in the poem. The draft existed to generate ideas that would be tested for probity and pertinence by his poetic discipline. Especially in the later poems these drafts were generative and suggestive rather than controlling, and one seldom finds drafts as detailed as those extant in the 1909–1913 diary so extensively quoted by A. N. Jeffares.[11] More frequently than not, the later poems begin without any prior prose draft. It may be that these drafts were made on scraps of paper now lost, but, since Yeats confided so much so systematically to his manuscript books, this seems to me a redundant hypothesis. The 1909–1913 manuscript books come out of a period when Yeats, in despair at the desiccation of his lyric power, was forcing himself in a deductive manner to the construction of works largely occasional in motive. And it is revealing that the most extensive drafts of his later years accompany either occasional poems or those poems of *A Full Moon in March* that by his own testimony were written out of the same fear of barrenness that motivated the 1909–1913 manuscript books.

Even when prose drafts exist, the consistent width between draft and poem indicates that Yeats was a more inventive and less ideological poet than is generally assumed. He did not submerge himself in the process of experience with the kind of trust that characterizes, for instance, the later Ezra Pound. He shaped rather than merely voiced the ideas and feelings that came to him in the accidents of experience, but the manuscripts do not reveal a poet performing acts of composition out of the stale habit of being a writer. Instead they display the coöperative action of craftsman-like knowledge, intense feeling, dramatic imagination, laborious thought, and passionate apprehension of immediate qualitative experience. Yeats thought of such an action as a reconciliation of opposites, a marriage of sun and moon, an approximation to Unity of Being possible only, perhaps, in the "marmorean stillness" of his study. Poetry for him was a transmuting process that liberated a man to the greatest realization of his possibilities, so that the reader too could participate in this celebration of human potentiality. To this end, no labor was excessive.

Two Dramatic Instances

Of the poems instancing the development of dramatic structure to embody a prior complex of idea and judgment, two striking examples are "After Long Silence" and "Among School Children." Both begin with a prior judgment, a formulated subject, and then strive to attain the dramatic design that gives the subject body. They both originate in the texture of daily experience and move from the simple observation of personal situation to a clear articulation of the human condition. Writing of "After Long Silence," John Unterecker remarks,

> Perhaps nothing can be said about the moving eloquence of "After Long Silence." Written for Mrs. Shakespear, the poem's precise statement of man's ironic anguish—impotent wisdom succeeding youth's ignorant passion—is an achievement that is both untranslatable and accurate.[12]

The poem takes its origin in a visit to Olivia Shakespear in October, 1929. It involves no complicated system of symbolic reference and grows immediately from a personal experience that Yeats formulated in a summary version of a proposed "Subject":

> Your hair is white
> My hair is white
> Come let us talk of love
> What other theme do we know
> When we were young
> We were in love with one another
> And then were ignorant.[13]

Equivalence in the first two lines, invitation in the third, rhetorical questioning in the fourth, followed by an implied answer. The syntactic method of this note would be denied in succeeding versions of the poem, so that in final form the poem becomes, by virtue of certain easygoing punctuation, a single sentence and stanza of eight lines. The direct address and personal admission of the initial two lines are lost, and the last three lines of this original notation are reduced to cryptic phrasing

Subject for "After Long Silence"

Versions of stanzas 7 and 8 of "Among School Children"

XII

Both nuns and mothers worship ima ges

But those the candles light are not as those

That animate a mother's reveries

But keep a marble or a bronze repose,

And yet they too break hearts - O Presences

That passion,piety or affection knows

And that all kinds of image symbolize ;

O self born mockery of man's enterprise.

VIll

Labour is blossoming or dancing where

The body is not ~~bruised~~ to pleasure soul ,

Nor beauty born out of its own despair

Nor ~~~~ wisdom out of midnight oil-

O Chestnut tree, great rooted blossomer

Are you the leaf the flower or the boler

O dance, seeing that all so smoothly runs

How small we know the dancer from the dance.

It seems the dancer and the dance are one.

June 14 1926

VI.

'Plato believed it all an idle play
upon the ghosts' images of things;
solider Aristotle played the taws
upon the bottom of the king of kings;
World-famous golden thigh'd Pythagoras
Fingered upon a fiddle stick or strings
What a star sang or careless Muses heard:
Old clothes upon old sticks to scare a bird.

VII

Both nuns & mothers worship images
But those the candles light are not as those
That animate a mother's reveries
But keep a marble or a bronze repose
And yet they too break hearts — O Presences
That passion piety or affection knows
And that all heavenly glory symbolise,
O self born mockers of man's enterprise.

VIII

Labour is blossoming or dancing where
The body is not bruised to pleasure soul
Nor beauty born out of its own despair
Nor bleer-eyed wisdom out of midnight oil
O chestnut tree great rooted blossomer
Are you the leaf the blossom or the bole?
~~O body ~~
~~O ~~ ~~glittering~~ glance
How can we know the dancer from the dance?

O body swayed to music, of glittering glance

86

that leaves the final "ignorant" in an aura of suggestive ambiguity. The complexity of the final version comes from forces that tug in opposing directions, so that the price of wisdom and the value of love are poised against each other in anguished doubtful balance.

He showed the draft to Mrs. Shakespear and eventually sent her the final version, but the poem did not emerge easily. At first he made some very tentative notes:

    a. Your other lovers being dead and gone
    b. Those other lovers being dead and gone

The first draft of the line had the tone of accusation, and he felt possibly the need for establishing equality and community between the two aged lovers. He made some essays toward end rhymes:

    friendly light
    hair is white

He then tried once again to phrase the theme of their discourse:

    on love descant

But he crossed this out and rephrased what, as he contemplated the subject, seemed the main burden of the poem:

    a. Upon the sole theme of art and song
    b. Upon the supreme theme of art and song
    c. Upon that theme so fitting for the aged; young
       We loved each other and were ignorant

With the conclusion reasonably clear in mind, he could then return to the poem's beginning and formulate an entry into its matter.

Taking up the whole poem once again, he employed a fresh phrase in place of the trite Irishism "dead and gone," a phrase that he could use ironically in the occasional public poem "September, 1913," but too flat for this poem of direct impassioned assertion.[14] Literalness evidently took precedence, and his courtly manner of greeting came directly into the poem:

> Once more I have kissed your hand and it is right
> All other lovers being estranged or dead

His notation remained literal as he struggled toward a clear notation of the remembered scene:

> The heavy curtains drawn—the candle light
> Waging a doubtful battle with the shade

And though the general idea and vocabulary of the concluding lines were fairly well settled, his next try left the fifth and seventh lines vague, repetitive, and prosodically ineffective:

> a. We call our wisdom up and descant
> b. We call upon wisdom and descant
> Upon the supreme theme of art and song
> Decrepitude increases wisdom—young
> We loved each other and were ignorant

The chief trouble with the poem that he then saw was the passage beginning with the candlelight and ending with the penultimate line. On the facing page of his manuscript book he made yet another attack:

> The candle hidden by its friendly shade
> The curtain drawn on the unfriendly night
> That we descant and yet again descant
> Upon the supreme theme of art and song

Returning, evidently in a completely different situation
when he had only a purple pencil with him, he made
the last of his imperfect drafts:

a. The friendly lamp light hidden by its shade
b. Unfriendly lamp light hidden by its shade

a. And shutters clipped upon the deepening night
b. Those curtains drawn upon the deepening night—

> That we descant and yet again descant
> Upon the supreme theme of art and song—
> Bodily decrepitude is wisdom—young

Once he had changed the friendly lamplight to an
enemy, he attempted to avoid the repetition of "unfriendly" by the use of "deepening"; ". . . shutters
clipped upon the deepening night" seems almost too
good to lose, but he sacrificed it, somewhat later. He
preserved the phrase "deepening night," however, in a
fair copy, characteristically underpunctuated, and still
far from the final version:

> Once more I have kissed your hand and it is right—
> All other lovers being estranged or dead
> Unfriendly lamplight hidden by its shade
> The curtains drawn upon the deepening night—
> That we descant and yet again descant
> Upon the supreme theme of art and song—
> Bodily decrepitude is wisdom—young
> We loved each other and were ignorant

The suppression of the probably literal hand-kissing
permitted the extraordinary opening line to emerge,
with its long pause indicating the emergence of the
speech and the declarative assertion of the rightness of
conduct that is persistent in courage as well as deep in

anguish. The unfriendliness of both light and dark, life
and death, to the very old appears in sudden boldness,
and the flatness of "Bodily decrepitude is wisdom" becomes assertive rather than deferentially parenthetical:

> Speech after long silence; it is right—
> All other lovers being estranged or dead,
> Unfriendly lamp-light hid under its shade,
> The curtain's drawn upon unfriendly night—
> That we descant and yet again descant
> Upon the supreme theme of art and song:
> Bodily decrepitude is wisdom; young
> We loved each other and were ignorant.

In the final version "curtain's" became "curtains," the
punctuation was strengthened, and the title was, for one
printing, "Words After Long Silence." [15]

The crucial line, in readings of the poem, has always
been "Upon the supreme theme of art and song," all
printings of which have capitalized Art and Song. Perhaps the capitalizing has been one source of confusion,
so that Brooks and Warren have read the line as "Art
and song *are* the supreme theme," only art and song
matter in view of the inevitable loss of bodily force, and
the ignorance of the young is wasteful.[16] This is a possible reading, but in view of the early versions of the
line, it seems considerably less supportable than the
commonsense reading: the supreme theme of art and
song is love. The variants of the line bear this out:

> Come let us talk of love
> What other theme do we know
>
> On love descant
>
> Upon the sole theme of art and song

> Upon that theme so fitting for the aged; young
> We loved each other and were ignorant.

And though it might be argued that he changed his mind in the midst of composition, this seems to me extremely doubtful.

The poem begins with the outlines of a situation and the statement of an idea, written down in linear form. The movement from general idea and situation is then back to the experience, where in the intermediate stages of composition, the literal circumstantial detail is brought to attention: the candle, the curtains, the shutters, the kissing of the hand. And with this urge toward the originating situation goes also a desire to evaluate, the insistence on the friendly candle, which first wages a "doubtful battle with the shade," an indication that "shade" entered the poem in association with its rhyme word "dead," and that at first it came to his mind because of its suggestion of shadow and spirit. The candle at this stage was the spark of life, the light asserted against the deepening surrounding dark, night, death. Even when he came to see the shade as a piece of furniture and not menacing—"The candle hidden by its friendly shade"—the shade was friendly, protective, to the flickering uncertain light, just as the room was friendly to the aging lovers, shutting out briefly their impending death and protecting their fragility.

Then suddenly the candle became a lamp, and with this act it was possible to see it not as the analogue of life but, with its persistent electric revealing glare, as the enemy to the illusive memory of youth, the harper on bodily decrepitude. So the shade became friendly

to the lovers and the lamplight unfriendly, a reminder
of death as surely as was the night. Once this was seen,
it was possible to effect the startling balance of the
equal unfriendliness of night and light. The pattern of
composition displays first an abstraction from the experience followed by a return to the experience, followed
in turn by yet another abstraction that would deny the
actual setting and action, the kissing of the hand and
the candle. The setting was more literary than the en-
suing poem.

The poem represents a controlled reduction of complexity and a refusal of invitations offered by fact and
possibility. The ability to refuse the blandishments of
"deepening night" and the pathetic candle in favor of
the grand denials of the third and fourth lines exem-
plifies a kind of discipline that was Yeats's great
strength. The process of movement from abstraction to
immediacy to poetic embodiment is deliberate and
full of artifice, second and afterthoughts, condensations
and omissions, restraints and delicacies. The role of the
poet in this process is one of humility before the
emergent poem without self-abasement, honesty without self-indulgence. In the attainment of personalism
he skirts the self-characterization that he thought of as
egotism, most notably in the censoring of his own
courtly habits. The process of composition shows in
miniature the sort of problems that Yeats faced and
triumphantly solved in shaping dramatic matter from
his most deeply intimate experience.

"Among School Children" is a more elaborate structure that reveals some of the same characteristics noted

in "After Long Silence." Its extensive structure and its richer iconographic surface, however, reveal other aspects of Yeats's habits of composition. The poem has its germ in a judgment already firmly established in Yeats's mind:

> Topic for poem—school children and the thought that life will waste them, perhaps that no possible life can fulfill their own dreams or even their teacher's hope. Bring in the old thought that life prepares for what never happens.[17]

The "old thought" had appeared before in the *Autobiography* and *At the Hawk's Well,* and it had come forcibly to his awareness during a Senatorial visit to an elementary school.[18] But in the final poem this notion is only one among many that are folded together in a design of meaning much more complex than this brief statement would suggest. As he contemplated the school children, they became merely a part of the totality of life and death, in fact an occasion for a series of meditative pronouncements on an entire range of antimonies of which age and youth proved to be only a small part. With the poem more fully developed, he wrote to Olivia Shakespear that the poem was a curse upon old age:

> Here is a fragment of my last curse upon old age. It means that even the greatest men are owls, scarecrows, by the time their fame has come. Aristotle, remember, was Alexander's tutor, hence the taws (form of birch)

> > Plato imagined all existence plays
> > Among the ghostly images of things;
> > Solider Aristotle played the taws
> > Upon the bottom of the King of Kings;
> > World famous, golden thighed Pythagoras

Fingered upon a fiddle stick, or strings,
What the star sang and careless Muses heard.—
Old coats upon old sticks to scare a bird.

Pythagoras made some measurement of the intervals between notes on a stretched string. It is a poem of seven or eight similar verses.[19]

His indeterminacy about the length of the poem is, as we shall shortly see, one of the major forces that compel the final version of the poem to certain ambiguities. I would suggest that Yeats really did at one point intend the poem to be a blend of curse and lament upon old age and that the famous concluding stanza was not part of the poem's intended shape until very late in the process of writing. This accounts for certain very curious qualities in the last two stanzas. "Among School Children" is the ultimate proof of the fact that in Yeats the terms "genesis," "basis," and "final form" are only very distantly related.

Beyond the germinal note and the letter to Mrs. Shakespear, little remains in Yeats's notes to suggest the initial impetus of the poem. A single page of scribbles suggests that he began to explore the theme of disappointed possibilities, and in those notes he eddied around the substance of stanza five.[20] He left these notes behind, however, and entered directly into the poem. The first stanza moved easily to its final form except for some hesitation in line 5 as to whether the children learned to mend, clip, or cut, and his use of "histories" rather than history (this persisted through early printings). The second stanza also moved directly to its familiar shape except for hesitation at line 3, where "Told of a passing trivial event," a mechanical articulation, existed briefly before being replaced by "Told of a harsh reproof, or trivial event." The last line temporarily invited heavy stress on two prepositions ("Into the yoke and white within a shell") with no syntactical justification, and this quickly was changed to "Into the yoke and white of the one shell." His spelling of "parabel" or "parabell" for "parable" persisted through the poem's printing in the *Dial,* and it is an interesting revelation of how he actually pronounced the word. The third stanza also differed little from its final form, only line 3 causing any trouble, existing in its first version as "And wonder if she stood so at that age." Most of the manuscript variants in the first three stanzas were lines articulated without the accumulation of heavy stress that was, in such poems, his primary prosodic motive: "In poetry, every word matters."

Only in the fourth stanza do his difficulties become oppressive and exacting. The first line went through two versions:

    a. Then her present image floats to mind;
    b. Her present image floats into mind;

Even the second version is palpably defective, lacking a syllable (*"the* mind" in all printed versions and later in the manuscript). The second line existed in one hopelessly confused version, which was evidently rescued and reshaped for the printed version of the poem in the *London Mercury:*

    a. As ~~Time~~ da Vinci crayon fashioned it
    b. What Quintocento finger fashioned it

Version "a" became "Da Vinci finger so had fashioned it" and "b" "What quinto-cento finger fashioned it" un-

til he settled on "Quattrocento." Later in the stanza
Yeats came up short on the problem of presenting his
own image:

> And I—though never of Ledean kind
> a. Had certain points—there is torment in that thought
> b. I even I—that were a stupid thought
> c. Have wrongs to brood upon—enough of that

This unusual instance of self-pity persisted through the
poem's printed appearance in the *Dial*.

With this single exception, then, the first four stanzas
seemed to move easily and naturally toward their final
form, and Yeats's fluent presentation of the naturalistic
framework was troubled by few of the second and afterthoughts that we observed in "After Long Silence." The
easy and gracious movement of observation and reflec-
tion was a largely pleasurable notation, and the movement of the verse generally displayed a bravura that,
in many of the later manuscripts, shows the secure
pleasure of his control over the idiom of verse. Difficulties appeared only when he came to the assessment
of his current being and increased as, in the last half
of the poem, he became increasingly subjective and
overtly symbolic.

Although the initial notes for stanza 5 are extremely
unformed and—even for a Yeats manuscript—illegible,
their idea is clear enough, and the first half of the poem,
in its seemingly casual course, had been moving toward
it with intent. The implied matter of the first four
stanzas is the soul's loss on its entry into the flesh, and
the various oscillations from youth to age, child to nun,
child to aging man, learning to innocence, play to
wisdom, the present to the conjectured past childhood

image of the lover—all these prepared the way for the questions to be overtly examined in stanza 5, much as the parable of the egg suggested a lost primordial unity to be approximated in passionate affection. So the sense of loss that is one dominant thread of the poem has been paralleled by possible unity, and the poem in its last half can treat these themes by moving beyond the limited range of observation and experience to suggestions of universal order and application.

The initial notes for the poem, after the brief statement of germinal idea, are also the notes for stanza 5. Although certain words are illegible, it is clear enough that the beginning scribbles were concerned with the soul's betrayal into the flesh, still half-remembering its high origins. The mother, realizing all the despair "Of the soul betrayed into the flesh," would not, if granted a vision of "The image that the child would be in sixty years," think such an outcome adequate compensation. This judgment, as well as the general ottava-rima stanzaic scheme, was established very early, almost certainly before the rest of the poem was started. Arriving at the point in the poem where this theme was to be overtly stated, Yeats still had to seek out the appropriate icons and diction. The search resulted in troubled syntax leading to ambiguity and unclarity that Yeats hardly intended. His first effort was, as usual, very sparsely punctuated, and I have added parenthetically the minimal punctuation necessary to the sense:

> What youthful mother, rocking on her lap
> A fretful thing that knows itself betrayed
> And struggles with cruel demons to escape
> Before its memory and apprehension fade(,)

Would think—had she foreknown that shape(—)
Her son with sixty winters on his head
A compensation for the pang of his birth
Or the uncertainty of his setting forth(.)

This expresses the general Hermetic and Neo-Platonic view of the role of the daimon in bringing the soul to bodily existence, in which view the soul struggles to retain its memory of former glory, and this view of transcendent reality is here integrated with the naturalistic sense of disappointment at the failure of the dream for ourselves and for those we love.

As he continued working on the stanza, Yeats was most troubled by lines 2 to 4, which in this version are vague and lacking in suggestion. The concept of the sweetness of the honey that traps the unknowing soul he took from Porphyry (see Yeats's notes to the poem) and stretched slightly to cover both generation and oblivion. In the first version of line 2 the honey is "oblivious," in its seldom employed sense of "causing to forget," but the second version of the line made the honey generative:

> a. A thing, the oblivious honey has betrayed
> b. A thing, the generative honey had betrayed

Moreover, in the first extensive draft, the "fretful thing" had merely "struggled," and though the disdain of "thing" was intended and all versions of the line minimized any emotional associations with the infant, he did want the child to be physically active. So the third line went through several versions:

> a. And that shrieks out and struggles to escape
> b. And must sleep or struggle to escape
> c. And that must sleep, shriek, struggle to escape

This last is the final version of the line in all printed versions, and at this stage its reference to the "thing" (later a more vivid but no less emotionally neutral "shape") is clear because of the syntactic parallel to ". . . that knows itself betrayed." Later when the syntax dropped the original ". . . that knows itself betrayed" to "Honey of generation had betrayed," line 3 would float without a referent and has understandably been joined by some readers to the mother in line 1.

The three versions of this (third) line also display a conflict between linear and rhetorical sense. The first version moves in a single direction, "shriek" and "struggle" being variants of a single emotional reaction, but the second version presents two alternative modes of conduct, sleep and forgetting of past glory (the "drug" of later versions of line 4) or a struggle out of generation and toward remembered blessedness ("recollection" in line 4). Sleep and struggle implied recollection and drug, but Yeats evidently felt that a line reading "And that must sleep or struggle to escape" would be a dead line in the movement of the poem, so that the substitution of "shriek" for "or," though it blurred the abstract parallel design between lines 3 and 4, was justified by its prosodic and dramatic density. The sense of the line took over his motivation, as it had to the detriment of syntax in line 2, and the mere rhetoric of the poem took second place to its poetics.

In this crucial stanza Yeats had difficulties that were in part semantic but largely prosodic in their bearings. The fourth line reveals a characteristic process; that is, it begins with a predetermined rhyme word which is modulated from perfect rhyme to assonance as the de-

mands of meaning require. He began writing the line
with commitment to "fade" as rhyme for "betrayed" and
wrote three versions of the line before shifting to the
half-rhyme of "decide":

> a. Before its memory and apprehension fade
> b. Before ~~the~~ its memories of its freedom fade
> c. As the drugged memories gleam or fade

The first two versions of the line were prosodically impossible, their movement involving many flat syllables
justifiable only mechanically, and the third version was
one or two syllables short (depending on whether he
followed his habit of eliding such words as "memories"
to "mem'ries"), and surprisingly "romantic" in the manner of his own early poetry. After dropping the rhyme
word "fade" and accepting the more active (more de-
cisive) "decide," he had still to make several trials before arriving at the final version:

> a. As still that half drugged memory decide
> b. As its drugged memory may decide
> c. As flitting memory or the drug decide
> d. As sudden memory or the drug decide
> e. As recollection or the drug decide

The remaining four lines of the stanza went through
no especially revealing changes, other than some syntactical revisions of lines 5 and 6, and the last two lines,
so close in phrasing to the notebook description of the
subject, were never altered from their first appearance
in the manuscript. When a fair copy of the stanza was
typed up from the scribbled-over manuscript, Yeats was
very close to the final version:

> What youthful mother, rocking on her lap
> A thing the generative honey had betrayed

And that must sleep, shriek, struggle to escape,
As recollection or the drug decide
Would think her son, could she foreknow that shape
With sixty or more winters on its head,
A compensation for the pang of his birth
Or the uncertainty of his setting forth?

The struggles and rejections that appear in the prosodic details of this stanza, where the texture of the verse moves away from the immediately perceptual and reminiscent toward the speculative and rhapsodic, become from this point on more gross and obvious.

Stanza 6 existed in a separate version that obviously preceded the versions in the previous manuscript. In it the sense of line is rudimentary, displaying Yeats's prosody before it had reached the tight control typical of more advanced versions:

Caesar Augustus that made all the laws
And the ordering of cverything
Plato that learned geometry and was
The foremost man at the soul's meaning
a. That golden thighed far famed Pythagoras
b. World famous, golden thighed Pythagoras
Who taught the stars of heaven what to sing
And the musicians how to measure cords
Old clothes upon old sticks to scare the bird

Only lines 5 and 8 are even close to the form that they would have in the final version, and Augustus would disappear entirely, to be replaced by Aristotle and Alexander. The stanza exhibits a reasoned rhetorical order, from the individual soul as seen by Plato to the state as organized by Augustus, to the universe as directed by Pythagoras, a widening circle of meanings. Provisionally, it granted structure. But Yeats was not so centrally concerned with temporal organization as this ordering would indicate, and his basic contempt for merely civil authority was to lead, in the final version, to Aristotle's cavalier treatment of Alexander. The "ordering of everything" that he ascribed to Augustus became Aristotle's achievement in his next effort, and Pythagoras became describer rather than tune-setter of the universe:

a. Plato had measured the souls weight and poise
b. Plato pronounced upon the weight and poise

a. Described its horses, and what breadth of wing
b. Of the souls horses, and what breadth of wing

a. Such shoulders carry; Aristotle was
b. Carried them skyward, Aristotle was
c. Climbs heaven quickest; Aristotle was

> The first who had a place for everything
> World famous golden-thighed Pythagoras
> Proved by measurements on a fiddle string
> What music the empyrean dancers heard—
> Old clothes upon old sticks to scare a bird.

And even with Augustus omitted and Pythagoras given a more modest role, the stanza did not satisfy Yeats: the description of Aristotle was banal to the point of being foolish, and the detail of the soul's horses brought in confusing associations and could hardly bear the burden of summarizing the great Platonic innovation. In the following draft of the stanza he sought to summarize Plato's insights and, by giving Aristotle dominance over the temporal power, insist on the forceful pretensions of the human intellect. By the time of this rewriting, he had evidently decided to use the image of the dancer in his final stanza, and the "empyrean dancers" or stars had to be excised as a source of possible confusion:

a. The human intellect, cried Plato, plays
b. Plato thought the intellect but
c. Plato believed that all existence plays
d. Plato imagined that existence plays
e. Plato imagined all existence plays

a. Upon the ghostly images of things;
b. Among the ghostly images of things;

a. Solider Aristotle laid the taws
b. Solider Aristotle played the taws

    Upon the bottom of the King of Kings;

a. World famous gold thighed Pythagoras
b. World famous, golden thighed Pythagoras

a. Had fingered out on fiddle stick or strings
b. Fingered upon a fiddle stick or strings

a. What the star sang and careless Muses heard
b. What a star sang and careless Muses heard

    Old clothes upon a stick to scare a bird

All these magniloquent activities add up to wonderful indolence, underlined by the boldness that allowed Yeats to insist on "played" in line 3 rather than "laid," so that there is a sense of accomplishment and pointlessness to the wide range of human thought rendered in the stanza. The last line seems both a verdict on the processes described and a laconic summary of what the stars sang. But the verdict has already been made by the beautifully controlled tone, the surprising cogency of the brief statement of Plato's thought, the apparent inevitability of "paradigm" (Thomas Taylor's favorite term for archetype or Platonic idea or essence), the sympathetic humorous dismissal of Plato, Aristotle, Alexander, and Pythagoras which does not seem patronizing chiefly because the poetic brilliance certifies Yeats's equality with the great. This easy natural meditation of a man at once engaged and amused has the same fluency as the first half of the poem in its gracious notation and reminiscence. But all this ease was the product of temptations refused and false lures denied:

> Plato thought nature but a spume that plays
> Upon a ghostly paradigm of things;
> Solider Aristotle played the taws
> Upon the bottom of a king of kings;
> World-famous golden-thighed Pythagoras
> Fingered upon a fiddle-stick or strings
> What a star sang and careless Muses heard:
> Old clothes upon old sticks to scare a bird.

This stanza prepared the way for the close of the poem, and, though the manuscript offers no absolute proof, I believe that the urbane, knowing tone of this deprecating treatment of ambitious intellectual effort originally prepared for a sorrowful and disillusioned conclusion.

The following stanza (7) was not in its first four lines very different from the established printed versions. "Both" in line 1 replaced the indefinite "The" of the first try, and in line 3 "animize" appeared briefly before "animate" took its place. He was uncertain about the material of the statuary, using metal, wood, and clay before deciding on marble and bronze as more appropriately dignified substances:

> Both nuns and mothers worship images,
> But those the candles light are not as those
> That animate a mother's reveries,
> But keep a marble or a bronze repose.

The last four lines, however, show an earlier meaning for "Presences" and in their earlier version suggest a completeness, a full stop to the experience of the poem:

> And yet they too break hearts—the Presences
> That love, or piety or affection knows
> And dead or living statuary symbolize
> Mock every great man and his enterprize

If Yeats had held to his original intention of writing a poem on naturalistic disappointment, this would have been a sorrowful and fitting ending, though the poem would have been considerably less than the version we know. But he did change the lines, and he did write the last (eighth) stanza.

In the final version of the poem the "Presences" can only be taken to mean the statues and children that are knowable by passion, piety, or affection, but in early versions the poet's prayer is directed to presences that are merely symbolized by the temporal figures:

> And yet they too break hearts—O Presences
> That passion, piety or affection knows
> And that all kinds of image symbolize
> O self born mockers of man's enterprize

This version expresses the concept of *correspondences*, the child and the religious image, as all earthly things, being mere spumes playing against a ghostly paradigm, echoing and reflecting the glory of the "Presences," who are self-born and accomplish their perfection without any labor on their part. In the final version the "Presences" merely symbolize heavenly glory, and are to be identified with the things below of the Smaragdine Tablet, and the only way to make sense out of the lines

is to assume that in line 5 the poet is apostrophizing
the temporal images, in line 8 the essences that they imperfectly embody. Really, however, the lines are explicable only if we assume a pentimento:

> Both nuns and mothers worship images,
> But those the candles light are not as those
> That animate a mother's reveries,
> But keep a marble or a bronze repose.
> And yet they too break hearts—O Presences
> That passion, piety or affection knows,
> And all that heavenly glory symbolise—
> O self-born mockers of man's enterprise;

The poem that might have ended with a brooding tone
of complaint is moving toward rhapsody.

The rhapsodic resolution of the poem (stanza 8)
eventuated in one of the great memorable apostrophes
of English verse, but the chestnut tree did not emerge
at once and easily. Although the first four lines of this
stanza required little reworking, the first line read in
the original version "All is blossoming or dancing
where," and the disdainful epithet "blear-eyed" for
wisdom appeared only after he had rejected "even,"
"clamorous," and "murky" and had tried "blear-eyed
knowledge," evidently feeling that wisdom did not necessarily arise from study. The last and climactic half of
the stanza, however, went through three distinct versions before attaining its ultimate shape. He began with
the rhetorical version long familiar to readers of the
printed texts:

> O chestnut tree, great rooted blossomer
> Are you the leaf the blossom or the bole?

But the first try at the concluding lines of the poem was
flat:

> O dance when everything's so finely done
> How can we know
> It seems the dancer and the dance are one

Evidently he had started to write "How can we know the dancer from the dance?" but suppressed it, possibly in the interests of rhyme. But he made another effort, using the line in spite of the very imperfect rhyme:

> O dancer, seeing that all so smoothly runs
> How shall we know the dancer from the dance

But when this version was typed out, he revised the passage by pen and altered it so radically that the tree changed its species and function and the single dancer divided into a pair:

> O hawthorne tree, in all that gaudy gear
> Are you it all or did you make it all;
> O dancing couple, glance that mirrors glance
> How can we know the dancer from the dance.

The first two of these lines exhibit a strange ambivalence, a depreciation of the tree's showiness combined with an ascription to it of godly force and identity. The "glance–dance" rhyme gave Yeats the clue to resolving the problem of the concluding couplet:

> a. O dance are footfall, shoulder, glittering
> b. O blazing foot, O glittering glance
> c. O body swayed to music, O glittering glance
> How can we know the dancer from the dance?

The first version of line 7 is difficult to account for, except as an abortive attempt, and the second version was at least a syllable short. Eventually he changed "glittering" with its metallic hysterical suggestions to "brightening," with its implication of increasing and

diffusing light. With this last stanza the problems posed
by the poem were transported into a world of transcendent possibilities, successes beyond the reach of the
divided life embodied in the first four stanzas of the
poem and in the aspirations of the great intellects. Two
of Yeats's favorite icons standing for unity of being, the
tree and the dancer, represented an integrity of parts
so welded as to make any abstraction from them impossible, dramatizing ". . . the flow of flesh under the
impulse of passionate thought" that he so admired.

This vision of heavenly glory—and the temporary use
of the hawthorne tree suggests that he was talking of
something more than aesthetic quality (or taking
aesthetic quality to have a religious validity)—ends
with a question that is neither answerable nor rhetorical
but denotative of a desire, a fulfillment, and the impossibility of that fulfillment. The poem has, to that point,
inspected the modulations of the ambiguities of his experience and the tensions which they rouse, and it has
done so with an easy sense of spaciousness. Its moral
aim is to display those tensions as guides, not to action, but to contemplation of the nature of things, and
the ultimate outcome of such contemplation is the
aesthetic rationality that he saw as tragic. His protagonist moves from conflict to simplicity, ending in the
passionate apprehension of value. The apprehension of
value is an extreme measure that annuls for the moment
of apprehension the world to which it should refer. The
truth is embodied; it is not known; it is ambiguous and
dubiously attainable; it is the resolution of all opposi-
tions and the unity of all being.

For years, before studying the manuscripts, I had

been puzzled by the blurred reaction that I had to the poem, feeling that, in view of the many golden opinions it had earned, my reaction came from dullness. But I now think that the poem is clear to me, and in its clarity more interesting, a more integrated human drama. The "explanation" of the Presences of stanza 7 is minor, though it is surprising that the passage has troubled so few readers. The most recent comment, and a sensitive and informed one, by Mr. Unterecker, assumes that the Presences symbolize—stand for—all heavenly glory, so that the line "And that all heavenly glory symbolise" is not a break in texture at all, and a minor act of charity toward the poem makes that a perfectly acceptable reading. In fact, in Yeats's mind, and in the most detailed scrutiny of the poem's language, the Presences *are* all heavenly glory; they are symbolized by the worshiped images, and through such pious acts of passionate affection known.

This quibble, for it is little more than that, is suggestive, for it shows beneath the very slightly troubled surface brilliance of the verse an effortful illusioning. The process of composition that I see in the manuscripts involves on Yeats's part a determination toward exaltation and away from the tone of complaint that would have marked the poem if he had insisted on ending the poem with

> . . . the Presences
> That love, or piety or affection knows
> And dead or living statuary symbolize
> Mock every great man and his enterprize

Then the poem would have exhibited a collapsed morale, a denial of the very imaginative processes of which such poems are the product, analogous to Carlyle's unhappily paradoxical position of having written fifty books on the virtue of silence. It would have expressed the antirational bias so persistent in Yeats's work, and the nuns and mothers would have been seen as stronger and more enduring than Aristotle, Plato, Pythagoras, every great man (including the writer of the poem) and his enterprise. In this it is strongly reminiscent of the swan of "Nineteen Hundred and Nineteen" that leaped into a desolate heaven and brought the urge to destroy

> What my laborious life imagined, even
> The half-imagined, the half-written page. . . .

The innocent piety of these women would be established as the antithesis to the malicious surrender to evil of Lady Kyteler.

After *The Tower* appeared, Yeats expressed astonishment at the bitterness of the book, and in "Among School Children" we find him rejecting the bitterness attendant upon his mature and, as he evidently then saw it, testamentary comment on experience. Thus in the process of preparing the book for publication he rejected the self-pity of

> And I though never of Ledaean kind
> Have wrong to brood upon. . . .

in favor of the humorously self-dismissive

> And I though never of Ledaean kind
> Had pretty plumage once. . . .

This change symbolizes the kind of change that the subject of the poem underwent.

The originating "old idea" that life prepares for what never happens was not only germinal but fundamental to the poem. The comfortable old scarecrow, the shape with sixty or more winters on its head, the old clothes upon a stick to scare a bird were parallels to several other desperations uttered in the entire book:

> Everything that man esteems
> Endures a moment or a day.
> Love's pleasure drives his love away,
> The painter's brush consumes his dreams;
> The herald's cry, the soldier's tread
> Exhaust his glory and his might. . . .[21]

> . . . who knows no work can stand,
> Whether health, wealth or peace of mind were spent
> On master-work of intellect or hand,
> No honour leave its mighty monument,
> Has but one comfort left: all triumph would
> But break upon his ghostly solitude.[22]

But in "Among School Children" the desperation was not enough. The chief bitterness in *The Tower* seems to come from the earlier of the poems, especially the two great odes "Meditations in Time of Civil War" and "Nineteen Hundred and Nineteen." The end of the title poem, "The Tower," and the closing stanza of "Among School Children" were both written late in the great productive period of which *The Tower* is the key book. They mark a movement toward affirmation and away from the bitterness of the poems written during the troubles and the civil war.

The drama of the poem is in the willfulness of its motivation. Changing in his mind as he wrote, the poem shows distinctly the sense of dramatic possibility run-

ning the gamut from self-pity and brooding complaint
to dramatization of his historical being as representative figure to the ultimate identification of individuality
and character with the emergent symbol of the eternal
mind with which he and his audience can be identified
for the moment of contemplative grasp. Even the relative difficulty of articulation, the necessity for invention and fabrication and rewriting, increases as the
poem moves past its original motive to ultimate form.
An imaginative act takes over from an intellectual intent so that a relatively simple design of ideas is forced
to accommodate itself to a more embracing range of
thought and feeling. In many ways this process is emblematic of the working of Yeats's sensibility, his involvement in the observable movement of life in the
world, his equally strong bent toward placing his ob-
servations against the vast implications of the universe
where men are mortal gods and gods immortal men,
where images of the world can invoke and even control
the paradigmatic reality of heavenly glory. We see too,
as we saw more simply in "After Long Silence," the
tactful restraint that compelled him to excise references
to personal wrongs that he might brood upon, and his
reasons for complaining. There is a moving strength in
his power to turn from such self-pity to a humorous acceptance of his own absurdity as public man. It would
have been very easy to stop with a curse on his old age,
admit bad feeling, self-pity, and sickly remorse, and
the poem certainly does not deny or evade the indig-
nity of life. But, finally, in spite of the forced and
desperate passion of the last stanza, the poem embodies a nobility of bearing and a humane courage that

are admirable, noble, exalting, and even elevating. It is part of Yeats's greatness that he compels his readers to assent to the obvious—and therefore often forgotten —fact that one aim of poetry is to exalt through revealing the possibilities of life, not to idealize or improve upon but to show what, in effect, we might be missing. This motive seems to me the more deeply affecting, the more humanly touching, to the extent that we see Yeats having forcibly to remind himself of its importance when practically through with the articulation of a poem which, even in the projected first version, would have satisfied any but the greatest of poets. I am perfectly content with the final version, and I am not trying to substitute the manuscripts for the printed version; but there is in the manuscripts another variety of drama, that is, an action of puzzlement, self-analysis, revelation, lurching mistake, refinement, recovery, and ultimately triumph.

"Among School Children" is perhaps the most widely admired single poem by Yeats, and it shows in its final version and in its evolution in manuscript form several elements in Yeats's dramaturgy. It also suggests divergent motives in his verse, particularly in his iconography, which moves from the simple notation of naturalistic surface in the schoolroom to the enraptured apprehension of transcendent symbols. The sense of conflict and the movement of experience toward the climactic revelation that takes symbolic form is the primary surface that Yeats's later verse presents.

BETWEEN SYMBOL AND IMAGE

IN "Among School Children" we have seen something of the iconographic range of Yeats's verse, from the nuns teaching calmly and efficiently in the opening stanza to the nuns as symbols of all human desire in the closing portion of the poem. From the casual classical allusion to Leda to the revelation of symbolic tree and dancer, from the schoolroom to the Presences of eternity, from the general allusion to *quattrocento* painting to the obscurely learned allusion to the Neo-Platonic generative honey —the poem moves with practiced ease through all these levels of reference.

The iconographic range of "Among School Children" is typical of that of any extended poem by Yeats and of the body of his work. Any given image, for instance that of the swan, can be used to represent several different levels of iconographic reference, depending on

114

the dramatic mode in which the poem is operating. The swan of "Leda and the Swan" is presented as an absolute entity, its value identified with its existence: it is like nothing else and it has a universal meaning. In the prophetic context of the poem, its meaning is not questioned, and there is no "as if" involved in Yeats's presentation of it for our contemplation. At the other extreme of its use, in "Coole Park and Ballylee, 1931," the swan is presented as possibly a simile: "And like the soul . . ." The *like* and *as* similitude of this iconographic use is conditioned by the reminiscent and self-dramatizing motive of the poem, just as the immediately presentative force of the swan in "Leda and the Swan" emerges from its total context of prophecy.[1] In the second section of this chapter I will examine in detail the swan's various appearances in Yeats's poetry, but for the present I would like to examine certain general problems raised by Yeats's iconography, especially as they are treated in two excellent books, by F. A. C. Wilson (*W. B. Yeats and Tradition*) and Frank Kermode (*Romantic Image*). Mr. Wilson sees Yeats as a religious poet while Professor Kermode sees him as the chief flower of a particular literary movement, and the conflict between their arguments is especially illuminating.

The religion with which Mr. Wilson associates Yeats is "heterodox mysticism," most specifically Neo-Platonism as it appears in the works of Plotinus, Porphyry, Proclus, and Julian. He feels that for total explication of Yeats's poetry it is indispensable to refer to the structures of a symbolism antecedent and exterior to the poetry. This symbolism is drawn from Yeats's extremely wide reading in the philosophies of the Near and Far

East and his immersion in the occult tradition from which, in Mr. Wilson's view, he drew symbols that ". . . are all variants of certain central types, and these occur universally. They are the primordial images, from which the religions each draw their universal truth." [2] It is not exaggerating Mr. Wilson's arguments at all if one assumes that the validity of any iconographic use in poetry depends on the religious value of the icon and that this in turn depends for validity on longevity—at least antiquity—and width of occurrence. Mr. Wilson frankly describes the poet as decorator of received ideas traditionally associated with certain icons:

It has always seemed prudent to disparage Yeats as a thinker. And indeed there is much in the detail of his philosophy that one feels has appealed to the poet's, rather than to the logician's, eye; whatever in a faith is beautiful, or simply picturesque, is likely to find a place in Yeats's own system; and since beauty is not always consistent with probability, it may sometimes be hard to understand how he could have believed as he did. Here I think we have to consider both Yeats's idea of his function as an artist (which was as a decorative worker) and beyond this the nature of his personal vision. It is a very easy matter for the ecstatic to believe. We need not of course believe with him—in his elaborate angelology, for instance, or in his theory of a transcendental and divine intersexual love in heaven—but I can see no reason why the informed reader should be unsympathetic: a failure to sympathise with Yeats's position is usually a failure to understand. The highroad to proper understanding of Yeats's poetry lies through his symbolism, and this in turn requires a knowledge of the tradition on which it is based.[3]

This passage is a fair representative of Mr. Wilson's thesis, and there are in it certain curious premises: first, a conception of beauty as frivolous when compared to faith, belief, logic; second, a depreciation of the poetic activity when compared with something called "personal vision"; third, a cheerful separation of form and content, such as one might expect in an American Puritan of the seventeenth century.

The fruits and limits of this position become clear in Mr. Wilson's treatment of "Byzantium," in which he makes the daring reading of the poem as taking place after the death of its speaker. Believing as he does that much of Yeats's vocabulary originates in some traditional nonliterary text, he does not confuse the "image" of the poem with the conventional literary meaning of the term, so that he sees the "image" as "a lifeless automaton, projected by the spirit in its own likeness into the physical world, while the shade is a substantial personality, the purgatorial ghost." [4] As I will show later, this interpretation is hardly exact, but at least Mr. Wilson's immersion in Hermetic texts allows him to break free of the more common misreading. But in spite of the rewards gained through his intimate knowledge of the tradition of heterodox mysticism, Mr. Wilson loses through it as well. When he interprets the line "Hades' bobbin bound in mummy-cloth," for instance, he falls into the card-index associations and the essentially mechanical poetics that frequently mar his book:

> The phrase ["Hades' bobbin"] takes us back to the spool on which, in Plato's *Republic*, the destiny of man is wound; but I doubt if we should look to Yeats's words for any very precise symbolism: the line seems to me to be imagery; and Yeats's purpose is no doubt to suggest, by a horrifying image, the essential *lifelessness* of his automaton, a mere thing. It also helps him to establish the undercurrent of an Ariadne motif in the lines, since the bobbin can 'unwind the winding path'; here we remember Shelley's image for the return to the intellectual con-

dition, to enter which, living backwards through time, is to 'unwind the woven imagery / Of second childhood's swaddling bands.' The Ariadne motif gives us also a link with Blake (though Yeats inverts him):

> I give you the end of a golden string:
> Only wind it into a ball—
> It will lead you in at Heaven's gate,
> Built in Jerusalem's wall.

The phrase, then, is suggestive rather than meaningful, and so also no doubt is Yeats's 'mummy-cloth': as in 'All Souls' Night,' this detail seems largely decoration, intended to make Yeats's mentor seem ancient, repellent, remote from life. Here, however, there is an esoteric meaning also, if we care to take it. . . .[5]

The phrase *may* take "us" back to Plato and Shelley, but what it has to do with Ariadne is past me, and the insinuation that Yeats is consciously inverting the irrelevant quotation from Blake has no basis. More important, however, is the explicit distinction here made between imagery and symbolism, symbolism being precise and esoteric, imagery imprecise, suggestive, and (surprisingly!) not meaningful. "Imagery," in short, is "decoration." The same mechanical allegorical motive compels the extraordinary observation that "A starlit or a moonlit dome," so crucial to the motivation of the poem, is ". . . decoration rather than symbol," and that ". . . the 'night-walkers' song' (and perhaps the 'soldiery' too) are largely decoration to prevent the argument from seeming excessively abstract. . . ." In this theory of poetry, we have two distinct levels of iconography, first the precise symbolism with esoteric meaning, and second the decorative imagery that merely tricks the reader into accepting the argument and proper symbolism of the poem. I am not phrasing the matter derisively; no one could be more bald and hyperbolic than Mr. Wilson, who is simply not interested in poetry except as a sugar-coating for a pill that, he is convinced, is good medicine. Cotton Mather was no more explicit.

And the curious thing is that, in spite of the barbarism of his point of view and his incapacity for taking poetry on poetic terms, so that one gets the impression that the metrical divisions of Yeats's verse were perverse typographic quirks, Mr. Wilson has written a good book on Yeats's symbolism. For it is true that Yeats's poetry often does depend on the existence of a pre-structured symbolism, and that he frequently relies on the carrying power of the tradition with which Mr. Wilson identifies him. This is particularly evident in his later plays, and Mr. Wilson's arguments are most persuasive when he is speaking of *The Herne's Egg* and *A Full Moon in March.* The early poems also relied on relatively fixed patterns of symbolic association, so that under the aegis of the sun and the moon, for example, Yeats shaped what amounted to a table of usable associations, culminating in "Lines Written in Dejection" but persisting through his later verse as well. But the point that Mr. Wilson finds indifferent is that these symbols were set—in the poems—in newly created contexts and that these contexts shaped meaning to such an extent as radically to alter the icon's reference. To use the terms of I. A. Richards' *Philosophy of Rhetoric,* Mr. Wilson is interested only in the missing contexts not the surface context, that is, the other words of the poem. He sees the icons of the poems as divided in quality between the inert worldly, pragmatically present, and the dynamic superhuman, the true *raisons d'être* of the poetry.

The justification of this position, in the terms discussed in my opening chapter, is that Yeats himself often accepted the notion of preparatory naturalism that preceded the symbolic revelation, so that his multiple dramaturgy encouraged a multiple texture modulating with dramatic intent from, say, the oratorical stanzas of part I of "Nineteen Hundred and Nineteen" to the rhapsodic revelation of evil that prevails in the closing section. This habit of building to dramatic climax is certainly part of the surface and intent of the verse. But it is not invariably true that the symbols drawn from occult or Neo-Platonist sources have an overriding prestige. The tree of "Vacillation," for example, and the figure of Attis hung thereon, are in effect lampooned by the total poem, and the swan of "Nineteen Hundred and Nineteen" is so conditioned by its context that it loses the dignity and supernatural sanction with which its source endowed it. The poetry often takes attitudes toward the symbols of Mr. Wilson's "perennial philosophy," and those attitudes are not always flattering.

The habit of mind exhibited by Mr. Wilson is allegorical, and in spite of the greater sophistication of other critics, much commentary on Yeats seems intent on discovering the philosophical context of the icons. No one except Mr. Wilson, so far as I know, has overtly described Yeats as a "decorative worker," using separable and meaningless imagery merely to provide a Trojan horse from which leap the meaningful symbols once the reader's defenses are down. Yet the concern with

Yeats's "philosophy" rather than his poetics, his biography rather than his dramaturgy, has behind it a sense of the "true" meaning of any given Yeatsean structure, as if his verse were a form of evasion and refusal, so that his ironic treatment of *A Vision* or his deliberate denial of the ecstatic role in "Vacillation" is taken to be a form of shyness rather than the complicated expression of his mind. Yeats was capable of large leaps in attitude, thoughtful distancings, immediate affirmations, self-denials and self-indulgences on a rather grander scale than that of his critics. Even the critics most fully devoted to a strictly literary interpretation of his work are reluctant really to accept the curiosity and changeability of his being.

In part the confusions over Yeats's iconographic practice rise from the series of essays on symbolism, growing mainly out of his studies in Blake, that he printed from 1889 to 1899. They form a coherent theory of symbolism, and they are probably the clearest and most forceful expression of symbolist theory and practice written by an English poet who came to maturity in the closing years of the nineteenth century. They form an extremely useful commentary on Yeats's practice during the '90's, and they are also useful for understanding the motives of poems written from 1917 on. The chief thing wrong with the theory to be abstracted from these essays is that it is too coherent, too neat, too conventional. For example, this theory is anti-allegorical, and the assumption of critics is that therefore Yeats's practice was anti-allegorical. Nothing could be more misleading, as the discussion of the iconography of the sun and the moon (the third part of this chapter) reveals. The theory is also very Pateresque in its identification of the artist and his view with the artifact; as the discussion of Yeats's dramaturgy has shown, this was merely an intermittent motive in Yeats's later work.

Based on these essays, a point of view has emerged, especially in the studies of Professor Frank Kermode and the late Professor Donald Stauffer, that counteracts the extremely simple allegorical interpretation of Miss Virginia Moore or Mr. Wilson.[6] The chief assumption of this view is that each of Yeats's poems composes—is— a unique symbol, a perfectly self-contained and self-regarding entity, in which the poet attempts to present a single newly created organic form. In his extremely penetrating study, Professor Kermode assumes that Yeats's poetics is at root identical with the romantic concept of organic form, that the poem is, in all its parts, equal, and that the aim is to compose a single image—hence his title *Romantic Image*—rather than to communicate an idea or provide an attractive setting for contemplation: it is the object of contemplation. The poem is then its own context, and the only admissible extension of it is by reference to the general literary tradition in which it participates or—much more permissible—by reference to another artifact by the same artist. Yeats himself validated this notion when in 1901 he commented on the shortness of the notes to the third edition of *Poems:* "They are short enough, but I do not think that anybody who knows modern poetry will find obscurities in this book. In any case, I must leave my myths and symbols to explain themselves as the years go by and one poem lights up another. . . ."[7] This is perhaps even more true of Yeats than of other poets, and Professor Kermode's brilliant interpretation of the iconography of the dancer is eloquent testimony to the importance of the literary tradition to Yeats and the ground to be gained by studying the interlacing of meanings in Yeats's own practice.

The theory has great usefulness so long as it does not grow into a closed circle. The theory tends toward circularity and postulates a closed system of reference whereby the symbol refers to itself in order to form a more extensive symbol which in turn refers to itself. This is the ultimate in poetic purity. With Yeats, its usefulness ends at the very point where, to his mind, the greatest poetry begins, that is, at the point of prophecy and revelation, where the poem opens out on the great permanent realities, the dramatic ecology, of the universe. When he writes of ultimate reality that it "can be symbolized but not known," he is stating a counterpart to the guiding motive of his dramaturgy: "A man can embody truth but he cannot know it." Art embodies reality and makes a dramatic or symbolic revelation; it is not a closed system.

Yeats's work is more artful and open than either of these theories of symbolism allows. The range of iconographic reference is multiple, as is the range of dramatic reference, and the results are more jagged and troubling than the concept of the self-limited organic artifact indicates. The sophisticated surface, the bravura, the pleasures of recognition and repetition are constantly threatened by the unforeseen, the uncontrollable, the emergency. The poetry is full of lapses, evasions, postures, discoveries, interventions. The iconography shifts, blurs, turns to one level of reference, then another, without warning or cue. There is a residue of the extraordinary, the odd, the insoluble, of what Yeats himself would consider both the rag-and-bone shop of the heart and a majestic heraldry that moves between heaven and earth.

The Swan

Among the chief recurrent icons of Yeats's poetry birds certainly hold chief place, from the linnet's wings of "Innisfree" to the "Miracle, bird, or golden handiwork" of the Byzantium poems and the birdlike things of his very last poem, "Cuchulain Comforted." They attracted him from his solitary boyhood in Sligo, and their pride, beauty, and instinctive designs of conduct obsessed him to his death. They moved with ease between earth and sky, visible to human eyes and indifferent, occupied with patterns of being that fit the shape of the universe without taking thought. Of all the birds in his poetry, the swan is especially interesting because in using it Yeats literally hovers between symbol and image, between natural and supernatural reference. And it differs from certain other icons that are emblematic of his work because he exhausted its usefulness, banishing it from the last seven years of his poetry at the very time when he was concerned with a final convocation of person and icon that had major weight in his work. When he first wrote of Baile and Aillinn in 1901, the lovers had appeared to Aengus in the form of swans:

> That old man climbed; the day grew dim;
> Two swans came flying up to him,

> Linked by a gold chain each to each,
> And with low murmuring laughing speech
> Alighted on the windy grass.[8]

But in 1934, when the same two lovers appeared in the poetry, they did not take the shape of swans but appeared in human form:

> Here in the pitch-dark atmosphere above
> The trembling of the apple and the yew,
> Here on the anniversary of their death,
> The anniversary of their first embrace,
> Those lovers, purified by tragedy,
> Hurry into each other's arms. . . .[9]

And after 1932 the icon of the swan, which is so intimately associated with one's sense of Yeats's poetry, dropped from sight.

Early in his lyric poetry, the swans made an appearance very similar to that of the narrative *Baile and Aillinn* cited above. In "The Withering of the Boughs" (first printed in 1900), the swans were linked by golden chains and associated with a king and queen not specified or explained. In the poem's dreamlike atmosphere they were associated with a life of eternal contented drifting. The protagonist begins by describing his dissatisfaction with his aimless wandering and ends with a picture of an ideal life:

I know of the sleepy country, where swans fly round
Coupled with golden chains, and sing as they fly.
A king and a queen are wandering there, and the sound
Has made them so happy and hopeless, so deaf and so blind
With wisdom, they wander till all the years have gone by;
I know, and the curlew and peewit on Echtge of streams.
No boughs have withered because of the wintry wind;
The boughs have withered because I have told them my dreams.[10]

We are in the land of the dead where unrealized human possibilities can be lived out. Song, wisdom, fulfilled love—in this land what is offered is an apparently indefinite extension of realized temporal quality, in freedom. These swans are dreamlike and unnatural because their reference is to the fabled design of love that Baile and Aillinn body forth. The habit of reference here exhibited takes its origins in mood (nameless desire in reverie form) seeking objective formulation in fable provided by the energy of Lady Gregory, so that the basic desire for a life of aimless emotional wandering can be justified. The swans do not rebuke the poet; quite otherwise: they vindicate, by their achievement, the very pattern that he lives without success because of an uncongenial (time-bound) environment.

The swans are emblems of desirable life. Yeats uses them as norms of value, but they are qualified by their context to such a degree that their prestige can be depreciated by the quality of experience in which they participate. And far from being fixed and limited in reference, they can in one poem explicitly contradict their meaning in another. The icon of the swan enters the poems in various ways, with divergent suggestions in meaning that form a general family cluster but remain different not only in their implications for life but in linguistic function. In "The Wild Swans at Coole," for instance, the swans upon the water among the stones differ radically from the obscurely systematic swans of "The Withering of the Boughs," partly because Yeats's technical preoccupations in 1916 differed: here he is concerned not with reverie, longing, and dream, but with drama, thought, and perception. If a palace—as

Hopkins affirmed—should at least be a house, then this poem seems to urge that a symbol should at least be an image.

The difference in linguistic function, the shift from Lady Gregory's books to her lake, from prestructured associations to actual floating and flying birds, need not imply complete discontinuity. The icon of the swan seems, in most instances, to offer itself to Yeats at a moment of crisis that affects not only the mind of the poem's protagonist but also the natural and historical milieu. In "The Withering of the Boughs" the swans exalt the mind to a point beyond the limits of temporal experience; in "The Wild Swans at Coole" the swans appear at a moment of personal distress and in their brilliance rebuke and console the protagonist. The personal distress is measured by the literally sublime indifference of natural setting to the protagonist. The boughs are not withered but caught in a deathful perfection:

> The trees are in their autumn beauty,
> The woodland paths are dry,
> Under the October twilight the water
> Mirrors a still sky;
> Upon the brimming water among the stones
> Are nine-and-fifty swans.
>
> The nineteenth autumn has come upon me
> Since I first made my count;
> I saw, before I had well finished,
> All suddenly mount
> And scatter wheeling in great broken rings
> Upon their clamorous wings.
>
> I have looked upon these brilliant creatures,
> And now my heart is sore.

All's changed since I, hearing at twilight,
The first time on this shore,
The bell-beat of their wings above my head,
Trod with a lighter tread.

Unwearied still, lover by lover,
They paddle in the cold
Companionable streams or climb the air;
Their hearts have not grown old;
Passion or conquest, wander where they will,
Attend upon them still.

But now they drift on the still water,
Mysterious, beautiful;
Among what rushes will they build,
By what lake's edge or pool   . .
Delight men's eyes when I awake some day
To find they have flown away? [11]

There is no suggestion that those swans are part of any symbolic system, even if one takes Yeats's poetry as a systematic constellating of associated meanings: swan, crisis, natural desiccation of milieu, satisfaction beyond human attainment. For the rewards here suggested are diametrically opposed to those of the earlier poem. The human being is explicitly excluded, at any point in his possible life, from the satisfactions which are—with the possible exception of permanence—natural rewards of an undivided animal state. Yet even the apparently objective permanence of the swans' passion and conquest can be explained by assigning its source to the bruised mind of the protagonist, who looks on the swans as the antithesis of his lapsed condition. His motives intervene to endow dramatically the swans with qualities that they may not objectively have: their achievements are his failures, and there is no suggestion that his failures are anything other than wasted passion clarified and measured by the simple attainments of natural creatures moving without thought in a natural landscape.

Yeats's changes in the manuscript bear out the idea that the natural scene rebukes the protagonist, for as his grasp of the poem became firmer, he changed the manuscript at every point where he could heighten the overflowing fullness of life as contrasted with the exhausted man. In early drafts he wrote that ". . . the lake waters are low," only to change this stress on aridity to read that the swans are "Upon the brimming water among the stones," and even the trees, which bore neutral "foliage" or "colour" in early drafts, attained ultimate "beauty." These swans were to be given context not by any received design of fable or philosophic structure but by the dramatic state of the human figure, and toward that end the revisions of the manuscript steadily moved.[12]

The swan embodied natural values, and in very few instances was it not associated with sexual potency or satisfaction. Even at the close of Yeats's brief, moving play *Calvary,* the two musicians fold and unfold the cloth to a song that ends with an evocation of the companionable birds:

First Musician.

> Lonely the sea-bird lies at her rest,
> Blown like a dawn-blenched parcel of spray
> Upon the Wind, or follows her prey
> Under a great wave's hollowing crest.

Second Musician.

    God has not appeared to the birds.

First Musician.

        The geer-eagle has chosen his part
        In the blue deep of the upper air
        Where one-eyed day can meet his stare;
        He is content with his savage heart.

Second Musician.

    God has not appeared to the birds.

First Musician.

        But where have last year's cygnets gone?
        The lake is empty; why do they fling
        White wing out beside white wing?
        What can a swan need but a swan?

Second Musician.

    God has not appeared to the birds.[13]

In explanation of this apparently simple and explicit song Yeats ascribed to his persona Michael Robartes a symbolic interpretation of the swans, the geer-eagle, and sea bird: "Certain birds, especially as I see things, such lonely birds as the heron, hawk, eagle, and swan, are the natural symbols of subjectivity. . . ."[14] And Yeats continues, applying Robartes' symbolism to his song: "I have used my bird-symbolism in these songs to increase the objective loneliness of Christ by contrasting it with a loneliness, opposite in kind, that unlike His can be, whether joyous or sorrowful, sufficient to itself."[15] There is, in normal nomenclature, no necessary identification of self-sufficiency with subjectivity, and as Giorgio Melchiori observes, the symbolism of the swan is here ". . . merely described *a posteriori* and not effectively presented in the lines." [16] What we are really facing is a special use of "subjectivity": it is eminently not introspective, it does not involve inner feeling, especially not compassion, and it is associated with sexuality: "What can a swan need but a swan?" The iconographic use is close to that in "The Wild Swans at Coole," in which the swan is capable of passion but separate from the troubles of men. In the earlier (manuscript) version, the sexual passion was central, and the birds were located at Coole:

> Father swan and swan the mother
> Mount above Coole Lake and fling
> A white wing out by a white wing
> What need have they but one another [17]

And except for his omission of Coole Lake and the alteration of the last line to eradicate its very human associations (especially with the Gospel and Epistle of John), the final version of the song in *Calvary* remains fixed in the general habit of reference already observed in "The Wild Swans at Coole."

Unless the term "subjectivity" has an honorific rather than specifiable meaning, it seems singularly inappropriate. But the swans achieve, without intellect or imagination, the end which human beings can attain only by imaginative acts that might, in their turn, purify the human being to the state naturally available to the swan. The swans live, without taking thought, in harmony with the motives and forms of the universal mind, are in fact an expression of that mind. In this sense they exist in two related capacities, so that they can be subjective and natural at once; and since they are separate from the human being, with its need for salvation, they can be seen by the poet objectively, as "others." The poet's task is to exhibit and realize associations rather than exploit them, to create contexts rather than assume or evoke, and to give dimension and immediacy to the natural objective being rather than play on a context of fixed allegorical association.

The difference between the use of the swan in "The Withering of the Boughs" and its use in the song from *Calvary* and "The Wild Swans at Coole" is the difference between received decorative fable and realized dramatic perception. In "Nineteen Hundred and Nineteen" a different habit of reference is at work, for in this poem Yeats explicitly assigns to the swan the traditional meaning derived from the symbology of Platonism, the swan as the soul. Socrates says in the *Phaedo:*

> Will you not allow that I have as much of the spirit of prophecy in me as the swans? For they, when they perceive that they must die, having sung all their life long, do then sing more lustily than ever, rejoicing in the thought that they are about to go away to the god whose ministers they are. But men, because they are themselves afraid of death, slanderously affirm to the swans that they sing a lament at the last. . . . But because they are sacred to Apollo, they have a gift of prophecy, and anticipate the good things of another world; wherefore they sing and rejoice on that day more than ever they did before.[18]

Whether Yeats draws the icon from this passage or some later commentary or mere general literary tradition, he wants the sense of association with systematic supernatural order:

Some moralist or mythological poet
Compares the solitary soul to a swan;
I am satisfied with that,
Satisfied if a troubled mirror show it.
Before that brief gleam of its life be gone,
An image of its state;
The wings half spread for flight,
The breast thrust out in pride
Whether to play, or to ride
Those winds that clamour of approaching night.

A man in his own secret meditation
Is lost amid the labyrinth that he has made
In art or politics;
Some Platonist affirms that in the station
Where we should cast off body and trade
The ancient habit sticks,
And that if our works could
But vanish with our breath
That were a lucky death,
For triumph can but mar our solitude.

The swan has leaped into the desolate heaven:
That image can bring wildness, bring a rage
To end all things, to end
What my laborious life imagined, even
The half-imagined, the half-written page;
O but we dreamed to mend
Whatever mischief seemed
To afflict mankind, but now
That winds of winter blow
Learn that we were crack-pated when we dreamed.[19]

Unlike the protagonist of "The Wild Swans at Coole," the poet is here not merely an aged person lamenting his biological losses. The approaching night and the winds of winter are the end of a cultural process, and the poet speaks in his role as representative of the deceived longings of an entire civilization.[20] And the swan does not exalt and lift his heart. The wildness and rage that attend his contemplation of its freedom suggest to him a suicidal escape, and the desolate heaven that the swan accepts is no improvement. For the entire poem— this is only one of six sections—is concerned with the wastefulness of labor, the permanence of evil, the impossibility of escape, the implacable indifference of the universe to human aspiration and toil. The swan invites him to destructive negation and dramatizes a resolution that defeats the human and is perhaps self-defeating as well: the most that it can achieve is a brief self-knowledge, and the heaven it enters is desolate and possibly illusory. And this is consonant with the way in which the poem treats all human inventions, whether political, aesthetic, or philosophical, and including the comparisons and analogies of poet or philosopher.

If the term *image* is used in Pound's sense of an intellectual and emotional complex presented in a moment of time and the term *symbol* to include only those icons that are also part of a received symbology, then the third section of "Nineteen Hundred and Nineteen" and "The Wild Swans at Coole" seem to represent these two extremes in Yeats's iconographic usage. But we would be misled to accept so simple an antithesis. In Yeats's practice even the fixed and established meanings are radically—sometimes unrecognizably—altered by their created context. The swan of Platonic symbology is qualified by the context of historical lament and personal distress so that it becomes identified with human failure and in the midst of desolation offers only desolation. The received symbol fails to exercise its magic and has merely emotional impact: "That image can bring wildness. . . ." It becomes then an image, caught in a moment of time, limited, a point of concentration for emotional and intellectual motives. The swan loses its power of resolving difficulties precisely at the point where exaltation and destruction are identified in an indissoluble relation, that is, when the poetry becomes tragic.

When exaltation becomes a pure possibility and the absurdities and antitheses of experience are resolved, however, the swan can symbolize transcendence of temporal limits. The title poem of *The Tower* is one instance in which the swan holds to the confined meanings of Platonic tradition, for in this poem a temporary resolution is made of the conflict between temporal and spiritual experience. For if, as the poem affirms, our spiritual salvation depends upon the quality of sensuous experience realized during life, where is the conflict? Faith in art and love combines with pride in personal identity to vindicate abandonment to experience. Thus Yeats makes an inventory of the legacy that he would leave to the young and lists first the pride that he takes in ancestry and kindred:

> . . . They shall inherit my pride,
> The pride of people that were
> Bound neither to Cause nor to State,
> Neither to slaves that were spat on,
> Nor to the tyrants that spat,
> The people of Burke and of Grattan
> That gave, though free to refuse—
> Pride, like that of the morn,
> When the headlong light is loose,

Or that of the fabulous horn,
Or that of the sudden shower
When all streams are dry,
Or that of the hour
When the swan must fix his eye
Upon a fading gleam,
Float out upon a long
Last reach of glittering stream
And there sing his last song. . . .[21]

The swan is associated with the fullness of nature, and, as in "The Wild Swans at Coole," it offers itself to the poet when he is contemplating the winter of his years and a crisis in his spiritual life. This swan, however, is not one of many natural birds but is close to the unique symbolic swan that the moralist or mythological poet identifies with the solitary soul. And this swan represents not rebellious resentment of life but fulfillment, so that the desolation that "Nineteen Hundred and Nineteen" ascribed to heaven and earth has no relevance. The identical icon can be employed for emotional qualities diametrically opposed, and the tragic limitations of one poem can assert boundaries for the swan that the transcendent possibilities of another poem sublimely ignore.

"Nineteen Hundred and Nineteen" was completed in 1921, "The Tower" in 1925, and the essential reference of the swan to Platonic symbology is the same in both poems, whatever the very differing weight placed on it. Yet between these two dates, Yeats wrote a poem that has only the most general relation to the meanings established in the *Phaedo* and qualified by the swan's leap into the desolate heaven or drift on the last reach of glittering water. The swan of "Leda and the Swan" emerges from a supernatural realm, embodies a god, and descends upon the merely human circumstances of Leda. In the first drafts the stress is entirely on the godhood of the bird, and there is a marked difference between the octave of the drafts and that of published versions:

> Now can the swooping godhead have his will
> Yet hovers, though her helpless thighs are pressed
> By the webbed toes; and that all powerful bill
> Has suddenly bowed her face upon his breast.
> How can those terrified vague fingers push
> The feathered glory from her loosening thighs?
> All the stretched body's laid in that white rush
> And feels the strange heart beating where it lies.[22]

Yeats's chief difficulty came from the opening two lines, and before getting the poem in publishable form he made at least two other versions:

> The swooping godhead is half hovering still
> Yet climbs upon her trembling body pressed . . .

> The swooping godhead is half hovering still
> But mounts, until her trembling thighs are pressed. . . .

Gradually he came to stress the bird-like rather than the godly qualities of the swan:

> A swoop upon great wings and hovering still
> The bird descends, and her frail thighs are pressed . . .

Even the first printed version held some vestiges of his earlier stress on the godhood of the swan:

> A rush, a sudden wheel, and hovering still
> The bird descends, and her frail thighs are pressed
> By the webbed toes, and that all-powerful bill
> Has laid her helpless face upon his breast.

How can those terrified vague fingers push
The feathered glory from her loosening thighs!
All the stretched body's laid on the white rush
And feels the strange heart beating where it lies;
A shudder in the loins engenders there
The broken wall, the burning roof and tower
And Agamemnon dead.
                    Being so caught up,
So mastered by the brute blood of the air,
Did she put on his knowledge with his power
Before the indifferent beak could let her drop? [23]

This version is still far from the masterful poem as it is generally known. The swan hovering and descending at once is a symptom of the halting descriptiveness of the poem that annuls the sense of immediate implication that distinguishes the final version. "Webbed toes" sounds like silly circumstantial detail, and "the bird descends" is portentous beyond any need. There is no necessity for making the explicit antithesis of "frail" and "all-powerful," which is certainly clear enough in the action itself, the use of "laid" exhibits a kind of easy carelessness, and the stretched body is simply awkward, especially when juxtaposed with the uncomfortably stifling image of Leda's face upon the swan's breast.

Even in this version, which Yeats was shortly to find inadequate, we can see a stress on the supernatural *and* natural qualities of the icon, their common superiority to the human. Caught up, mastered, conquered by this passion, the helpless ambiguous human state is defined. The habitual associations that Yeats's poetry had made with the icon of the swan—crisis, mutability, the desiccated landscape—are transformed to the predicted murderousness of love and war. The human figure is if anything more helplessly passive in this poem than in, say, "The Wild Swans at Coole."

The sources of this poem in literary tradition and in various works of visual art have been brilliantly explored by Giorgio Melchiori. His conclusion is that the swan of "Leda and the Swan" comes out of this general aesthetic tradition and that Yeats's contemplation of the scene is only incidentally related to the ideas underlying *A Vision*. I would suggest that *A Vision* is at least in part based on this poem and on other, similar experiences granted Yeats in the process of poetic composition. Through the poetic act he evaluated the designs of meaningful life. His retrospective note on the poem shows his mind moving from an abstract judgment through a generalized relationship on to girl and bird:

> I wrote Leda and the Swan because the editor of a political review asked me for a poem. I thought 'After the individualist, demagogic movement, founded by Hobbes and popularized by the Encyclopaedists and the French Revolution, we have a soil so exhausted that it cannot grow that crop again for centuries.' Then I thought, 'Nothing is now possible but some movement from above preceded by some violent annunciation.' My fancy began to play with Leda and the Swan for metaphor, and I began this poem; but as I wrote, bird and lady took such possession of the scene that all politics went out of it, and my friend tells me that his 'conservative readers would misunderstand the poem.' [24]

So he shaped an artifact remote from his original formulation: ". . . bird and lady took such possession of the scene. . . ." The motives were not at all those of satisfying the structures of *A Vision*—almost certainly the section ultimately titled "Dove or Swan" did not yet exist—but motives having to do with the demands of the material before him. The conservative readers of the *Irish Statesman* would be more horrified by the presentation of miscegenation than by any latent political ideas, and the imaginative vividness of the poem defeated its original motive: to present vital political ideas to the emergent ruling class of Ireland. What could they have usefully learned from one of the great poems of the English language? Yeats himself, learning from it, could use it as one of the focal points for his long prose discourse on history that marks the conclusion and climax of *A Vision*.

At some time between August of 1924 and May of 1925, he rewrote the poem so that the stress on "bird and lady" occupied the entire scope of the octave.[25] The bird ceased to be "all-powerful," and the manuscript versions reveal a willed insistence on physical qualities. Leda's "frail" thighs become "white" in contrast with the "sooty webs" of the swan, and with the deletion of "that all-powerful bill" he could try various phrases to underline the animal nature of Leda:

> . . . her nape is in his bill
>
> . . . her nape caught in his bill
>
> . . . that white nape in his bill
>
> . . . her nape caught in that bill
>
> . . . her nape caught in his bill

In his effort to specify and vividly envision the scene he fell into momentary absurdity:

> The bird has fallen but is hovering still
>
> Leda can run no more . . .

And where can Leda run . . .

And what can Leda do . . .

And Leda staggers . . .

Above the staggering girl . . .

But even the comical nail-biting of "What can Leda do?" turned his attention to the lady of the action and led to the special "carnal eloquence" that distinguishes the final version, with thigh, nape, and breast placed against toes, bill, and breast, the beating wings above the staggering girl:

A sudden blow: the great wings beating still
Above the staggering girl, her thighs caressed
By the dark webs, her nape caught in his bill,
He holds her helpless breast upon his breast.

How can those terrified vague fingers push
The feathered glory from her loosening thighs?
And how can body, laid in that white rush,
But feel the strange heart beating where it lies?

A shudder in the loins engenders there
The broken wall, the burning roof and tower
And Agamemnon dead.
                     Being so caught up,
So mastered by the brute blood of the air,
Did she put on his knowledge with his power
Before the indifferent beak could let her drop? [26]

Tracing the swan through his various appearances, we can see in this poem an initial bald statement of his godhood and omnipotence that is then deleted until he becomes a bird with wings, webs, and bill. His potency is in his action and the consequences of that action, so that the single mention of his power accompanies his mastery, bruteness, and sexual satiation. What this poem does, in effect, is to compose the essential duality of the icon, making it at once a symbol of supernatural power and an image of natural force: ". . . the brute blood of the air." The tragedy of Leda is that she should be a battleground, that her descendants should also be helplessly caught between the natural and the supernatural, the human image being endowed with significance only insofar as it can participate in the life of nature and supernature. So she is at once dignified, exalted, and destroyed.

Yeats's last extensive treatment of the swan appears in "Coole Park and Ballylee, 1931," the first three stanzas of which he once thought of calling "Swan and Water." [27] The locale is similar to that of "The Wild Swans at Coole," and the qualities of the milieu have important resemblances: the season is wintry, the wood is made up of dry sticks, and the scene reflects the psychology of the protagonist. But the swan is solitary, close to the unique bird of "The Tower" or "Nineteen Hundred and Nineteen," and the context is not limited to the personal memory of the protagonist. He is presented not merely as a man grieving for his own wasted youth (I am over fifty years old) but as an aging man in a dying civilization (I am over sixty-five, it is 1932):

> Upon the border of that lake's a wood
> Now all dry sticks under a wintry sun,
> And in a copse of beeches there I stood,
> For Nature's pulled her tragic buskin on
> And all the rant's a mirror of my mood:
> At sudden thunder of the mounting swan
> I turned about and looked where branches break
> The glittering reaches of the flooded lake.

> Another emblem there! That stormy white
> But seems a concentration of the sky;
> And, like the soul, it sails into the sight
> And in the morning's gone, no man knows why;
> And is so lovely that it sets to right
> What knowledge or its lack had set awry,
> So arrogantly pure, a child might think
> It can be murdered with a spot of ink.[28]

In a letter to his wife Yeats said that this swan was ". . . a symbol of inspiration I think," [29] but he wrote the letter ten days before finishing the poem, and in those ten days the swan appeared to him variously:

> image of inspiration, of the minds brief light
>
> An image of the soul
>
> What better image of the minds brief light
>
> An image of the souls uncertain flight
>
> Or of the soul of creation and of light
>
> An image of the soul, creation and light

But such bald ascription of allegorical meaning could not long satisfy him. He turned to the swan as physical appearance:

> A swan, a something stormy white
>
> A writhing swan, thunder of wings so white
>
> Strange image? of the soul creature of light
>
> Declares the soul, a bird and yet a light
>
> A something sudden strange and stormy white.

And then tried identifying physical form with idea:

> A metaphor of soul so stormy white
>
> And what if soul is his winged light

> Metaphor a something stormy white
> Something sudden strange and stormy white
> A metaphor of soul: creature of light
> Soul is a living creature of the light
> A metaphor of soul, a something stormy white
> And this an emblem for its stormy white
> And like the soul it sails into the sky
> And like the soul it sailed in the sky [30]

The image of inspiration appeared only once and briefly and was excised extremely early in the composition of the poem. The movement of the revisions was toward, first, the relation between swan and soul (rather than the less inclusive inspiration or mind) and, second, a depreciation of the icon from the status of allegorical symbol to mere metaphor to ultimate simile.

This process was urged by the shape and genre of the poem, that is, elegiac reminiscence. For his reminiscent poems, expressing his personal attachments, old associations, fondnesses, identifications of a social kind, tend to employ icons with a certain prosaic phrasing, as if his abdication of the vatic position compelled him to less assertive iconographic practices. In this poem he reverted briefly to the persona of a dying man in a dying civilization which had given range and density to the poems of *The Tower*. The energy of the poem is low, its voice hushed, its movement so bound and curtailed in mournful declaration that it seems out of place in the remorse- and passion-ridden poems of *The Winding Stair*. Attempting to project the personal past as filtered through his present state, he limited the potential reference of the language at one point but attempted to extend it at the close of the poem. From this came confusion:

> We were the last romantics—chose for theme
> Traditional sanctity and loveliness;
> Whatever's written in what poets name
> The book of the people; whatever most can bless
> The mind of man or elevate a rhyme;
> But all is changed, that high horse riderless,
> Though mounted in that saddle Homer rode
> Where the swan drifts upon a darkening flood.[31]

The splendid rhetoric of this passage almost saves the iconography from seeming, as it is, arbitrary and compelled. For if we examine the last line in terms of the associative web of the poem, we have the soul drifting upon the darkening generated soul when the generated soul is at its highest point. Only an allegorical leap can save the poem, so that one might say that at death the soul is at its height; but what then is to be made of the soul drifting on the soul? Reminiscing, his mind moved in one set of associations, while his habit of symbolic design was working in another, so that the natural swan at Coole became associated with the unique swan of Platonic symbology, then both blended with the swans drifting under Sligo bridge with the evening flood tide.

He had great difficulty with this particular poem, as shown in the tense shifts of stanza two (stood . . . Nature's pulled . . . rant's . . . turned . . . break) compelled by rhyme requirements.[32] In spite of its occasional assertive power, the almost Virgilian ordering of the poem, and the memorable phrasing, the poem still bears the weight of its motivation, that is, to fill out a design suggested by its companion piece, "Coole Park, 1929." Yeats himself, looking at the fair copy of the poem when it still included the stanza later excerpted and printed as "The Choice," considered it in those terms:

> The poem might perhaps make together with the lines introductory to Lady Gregory's "Coole" a single poem. The lines from "Coole" headed "A flight of swallows" as dated. Stanzas I-II-III of present poem called "The Wood" or "Swan and Waters" stanzas IV and V called "The House" and VI and VII called "The Comment" or "The High Horse" or "The last romantics" [33]

This directive to himself, written when the fair copy lay before him, indicates his trouble on observing the divisibility of the poem, especially when contrasted with the earlier dedicatory "Coole Park, 1929." The poem was divisible, and one point of divergent stress appears in his use of the swan and, briefly, the bitter egotism of the stanza later excerpted as "The Choice":

> The intellect of man is forced to choose
> Perfection of the life, or of the work. . . .[34]

It would be perhaps more gratifying if Yeats in his last extensive use of the swan as icon had made a comprehensively successful summary of all the potentialities he had to that point explored through it. But its uses throughout his work were, as they clearly are in this poem, divergent, the poetics under which each use operates is divisible, and the multiplicity, the essential pluralism, of his capacious and versatile mind is visible here as in his dramaturgy.

His iconography has a primary urge toward a community of feeling, but it attains this end by diverse means. It is dramatically conditioned by the state of being in which a given poem is involved, the deathly "image" of "Byzantium," the representative "character" of "Nineteen Hundred and Nineteen," the character modulating toward "personality" of "Among School Children," the embittered individuality of bad feeling in several poems. The tone and consequent reference of the language weights and qualifies the iconographic use.

It is not mere perversity, a reluctance to follow the interpretation of Yeats's symbolism established in Donald Stauffer's very fine book, that compels me to insist on the diversity of reference in Yeats's iconography. I am rather attempting to enlarge the sense of the poetic medium in Yeats's work, demonstrating as explicitly as possible that his work is not composed of "symbols," and further—in general poetic terms—that the stress on the symbol as the equivalent of pigment in painting does not exhaust the materials of poetry. If one thinks of the symbol as the primary—even exclusive—material with which the poet works, the tendency is then to think of each symbol as given, even fixed. With a poet like Yeats, who is frequently allegorical in intent, the temptation to accept his iconography as establishing a settled pattern of associations can easily blur the actual surface of his work. I find it pointlessly confusing to identify the swan of "Leda and the Swan" with the casual joke of "Among School Children":

> And I though never of Ledaean kind
> Had pretty plumage once . . .[35]

And it is equally pointless to relate the swan of "Leda and the Swan" or "Nineteen Hundred and Nineteen" with that of "His Phoenix":

There is a queen in China, or maybe it's in Spain,
And birthdays and holidays such praises can be heard
Of her unblemished lineaments, a whiteness with no stain,
That she might be that sprightly girl trodden by a bird. . . .[36]

What Yeats is saying in these classical allusions is, in effect, "as we all know," whereas in "Leda and the Swan" he is invoking a presence that changes all we know. He is speaking from such differing perspectives that he is really speaking as distinguishable voices, and it is the voice, the persona, that is a usable instrument, a device that is part of the poetic medium.

If we think of Yeats as merely a symbolist or as expresser of his individuated being, we are off the center of his poetics. For years now it has been fashionable to depreciate Yeats as a dramatist, on the ground that he wrote "lyric drama," which I take to mean that he wrote short poetic plays on mythical subjects. If the term "lyric drama" is reshaped to "symbolic drama," and it is assumed that Yeats was always writing as a dramatist, then the discrepancies and divergences in the reference of his iconography can be brought into a coherent pattern. His use of the swan has an analogue in his dramatic employment of the persona of Major Robert Gregory, a persona that allowed him to explore a variety of ideas and feelings about courage, versatility, and death, much as the swan gave him a range for examining self-sufficiency, sexuality, the natural as opposed to the human, the contact of human and superhuman, the validity of the soul, the melancholy beauty of familiar scene, the attritive force of sheer biological aging. It seems to me little more than an academic exercise to collapse all these obsessions and indications of valued experience into a portable set of associations. Yeats's use of the swan was designedly multiple, and his infrequent ascription of allegorical meaning so explicit and clear as to be satisfied in its immediate context. In short, it seems to me that the icon of the swan suggests the inapplicability of either the allegorical or the purely literary interpretation. When the late Professor Stauffer made his summary of the swan's associations, he excluded "Leda and the Swan" from consideration and thereby gave away the weakness of the approach to the icon as a pure literary symbol. And certainly, as the above analyses show, the strict Neo-Platonic interpretation of Mr. Wilson would have equal difficulties. To make sense of Yeats's iconography, it is necessary to assume that he is making a dramatic exploration of reality that he takes as symbolically inclusive, that the dramatic context is the instrument of a spiritual quest from which emerge values and meanings otherwise formless, not embodied. Far from overriding the limits of experience, his icons are frequently dragged down by the dramatic quality of the structured work, as the swan–soul equation is in "Nineteen Hundred and Nineteen." Poems are, as Mallarmé's reply to Degas asserts, written with words, but in Yeats's poetics the words tend toward formulations that relate persona to icon and icon to line in such a way that each is changed by its participation in a design of symbolic drama.

The Sun and the Moon

In a letter to Sturge Moore discussing a possible cover design for the Cuala edition of *Four Years: 1887–1891,* Yeats first discusses the hawk ("one of my symbols") and then lists several of his chief icons: "My main symbols are the Sun and Moon (in all phases), Tower, Mask, Tree (Tree with Mask hanging on the trunk), Well." [37] The Moon (in all phases) provides the symbolic design of *A Vision,* and both sun and moon appear steadily and prominently in his poetry through *The Winding Stair.* Like the swan, they diminish in importance and frequency after 1933, and when they appear do so briefly and with little emphasis. Although the sun and the moon are more complicated in their relation to Yeats's personal experience as well as more crucial in the structuring of his symbolic drama, their use parallels that of the swan, ranging from simple allegory to equally simple notation and allusion, and in between these inert extremes making several synoptic and inclusive convocations of the associations subsumed under these icons.

In their earliest appearance, up to 1889, the sun and the moon were sources of decorative light, mood, giving atmosphere to the vague sentiment and wispy shy feeling of his earliest work. The sun would lay his chin on a gray wood or the poet would come upon a little town slumbering in the harvest moon. But in the poems of *The Rose* (1889–1892) the sun and the moon began to refer to more complicated psychological processes and were used to convey feeling more fully structured and weighted. From this point to about 1915, his sense of their possible function in his poetry expanded so that they were now allegorical, now neutral and decorative, now conventionally romantic. In 1915, when he was brooding over his earlier experience in order to shape his autobiography, he explored the sun and the moon in the various ramifications he had opened up in his work and thought, so that he could trace out and inspect their personal and extensively symbolic reference. Hence on the verso of a page in the first draft of his autobiography one can find the manuscript—not very different from the printed version—of his "Lines Written in Dejection":

> When have I last looked on
> The round green eyes and the long wavering bodies
> Of the dark leopards of the moon?
> All the wild witches, those most noble ladies,
> For all their broom-sticks and their tears,
> Their angry tears, are gone.
> The holy centaurs of the hills are vanished;
> I have nothing but the embittered sun;
> Banished heroic mother moon and vanished;
> And now that I have come to fifty years
> I must endure the timid sun.[38]

The composing device is the antinomy of sun and moon, which is resolved in a minor key by the poet's rueful acceptance of the "timid sun." The centaurs as composite beings imply a possible resolution—more desirable than that of the conclusion—of the problem posed as the primary cause of dejection. They represent a desired transcendent unity of temporarily discordant and incompatible entities.

The centaur appears at two crucial points in the

Autobiography, first as a symbol of art: "I thought that all art should be a Centaur finding in the popular lore its back and its strong legs." [39] In one sense the poem states that Yeats's art has lost its roots in the deep irrationality of folk belief (the frustrated witches, the lost dark leopards), so that he is left with nothing but the surrogate intellectual elaborateness of a desiccated civilization. The intellect (the sun) is embittered in its very ascendancy, feeling its incompleteness and lacking the courage of its reveries.

At this level the poem is perfectly clear and satisfying, but the symbolic structure, at once personal and suggesting some implicit objective system, is so characteristic of Yeats's iconographic tone that it bears further inspection. Yeats's iconographic practice has a quality of intimate allegory that makes it puzzling and attractive. This is in part deliberate and in part an inevitable product of his temperament. It is also a major source of his charm.

I would like to depart briefly from my regular procedures and explore some of the biographical sources of these particular icons. Yeats himself, especially in the *Autobiography,* expended considerable energy on explaining the weight and reference of the sun and the moon. At one point he wrote that after finishing *Rosa Alchemica* he felt that his style had become too elaborate and ornamental. On consulting a friend he was warned to avoid woods because they concentrated the "solar ray" and to stay close to water. Yeats was certain that his friend was speaking in the voice of ". . . my own daimon, my own buried self," [40] and this judgment was validated by his own prior familiarity with these ideas. He had learned from Mathers to associate solar qualities with all that was similar to the work of a goldsmith (elaborate, full of artifice, rich), whereas water meant lunar (simple, popular, traditional, emotional). He followed his daimon's advice, and after invoking the moon for several days he was rewarded by a vision of first a centaur and then a naked woman of "incredible beauty" who was shooting an arrow at a star.[41]

His dream, he discovered, had appeared simultaneously to others, but when he returned to his first adviser, he received an explanation too cryptic to be useful. When he sought out a London coroner, learned in the cabala, he found that the dream was part of the basic wisdom of the world. The coroner showed him two water colors, one of a centaur, and one of a woman shooting an arrow at a star; the star, on closer inspection, was really a little golden heart. The centaur and the woman were respectively the elemental and divine spirits of the path Samekh, ". . . and the golden heart is the central point upon the cabbalistic Tree of Life and corresponds to the Sephiroth Tippereth."[42]

The Sephira Tippereth was attributed to the sun and was joined to the Sephira Yesod (moon) by a straight line (Samekh) attributed to the constellation Sagittarius.[43] In his main source, MacGregor Mathers' *Kabbalah Unveiled,* Yeats could find that the Sephiroth occurred in groups of three, one pair of opposing sexes, and a third uniting intelligence which was the beam joining the two scales of the balance.[44] The composite centaur was thus a convenient symbol for balance, as it is in "Lines Written in Dejection." In addition to the regular trinity, there was a single mighty one that com-

bined the King (Tippereth or Beauty) and the inferior
Queen (Yesod or Foundation) with the Crown (Ke-
ther), and ". . . the earthly correlatives of these will
be the primum mobile, the sun and the moon." [45] Joining and balance were the primary aims in effecting the
godlike, whether in religion or art or dramatic psychology.

What we have here seen in the obscurely systematic
terms of the occult Yeats saw also in the structure of
his family life. The duality of his heritage had been
plain to him from his earliest years: "Did not the Egyp-
tian carve it on emerald that all living things have the
sun for father and the moon for mother, and has it not
been said that a man of genius takes the most after his
mother?" [46] In his own parents he could see a pair of
strikingly complementary beings. His father was, as
his commentaries cited above indicate, an abstract
theoretician whose distinctions and pronouncements,
never really systematic and often violently in discord
with one another, dominated Yeats's early life and
thought and so affected his basic disposition toward
experience that in later years he would attribute the
origin of his aesthetic theories to John Butler Yeats.
Mary Pollexfen Yeats, on the other hand, was quiet and
gentle and evidently rested her being on a few simple
emotions and attachments. Whereas his father read
selections from Balzac to the child as a criticism of life,
she told him Irish fairy tales and spent hours in the
kitchen with an old servant, exchanging ghost stories
before the hearth. Her nature, at once passive and emotional, rooted in the country and past of Yeats's childhood, stood as complete antithesis to the restless

urgency of his father's distinctions, arguments, and cosmopolitan ambitions. Bringing the Hermetic and cabalistic symbols to bear on his personal identity, Yeats could use his own father to represent the elaborate art of the Pre-Raphaelites, the logic-chopping of John Stuart Mill and his followers, the whole of cultivated Europe with its civilized intentions and artifices. His mother could represent a certain nonintellectual and nonpolitical Irish nationalism, the folk tradition, the passive and emotional, the culture of Ireland as contrasted to the civilization of Europe. Ruminating on the problem of unifying culture and civilization, he wrote, "I myself imagine a marriage of the sun and moon in the arts I take most pleasure in." And the only praise which genuinely elated him to the point of turning his head was his father's statement that "We [the Yeatses] have ideas and no passions, but by marriage with a Pollexfen we have given a tongue to the sea cliffs." [47]

It is obviously not reasonable to assume that all these ideas were clearly present to his mind when he wrote "Lines Written in Dejection." They were, however, present in more or less fixed form during the period in which he wrote the poem, and the cryptic verses expressed a crux in his life through symbols weighted with intimate and allegorical reference. The dejection came out of his total life, worked back into his life, and had a cosmic background as well as an historical and biographical. The symbolism of sun and moon incorporated a long series of associations, beginning with alchemical and cabalistic reference and including his most personal motives and attachments. I propose the following table with a sense of reserve, and I am not

suggesting that the poem is to be read with any mechanical insistence on its relevance. I would suggest,
however, that it represents one instance of that special
tone of intimate allegory that haunts and tantalizes
Yeats's readers.

Sun	*Moon*
Beauty	Foundation
Male	Female
Father	Mother
Europe	Ireland
Cosmopolitanism	Nationalism
Civilization	Culture
Artificial	Natural
Elaborate	Simple
Rational	Emotional
Individualistic	Popular (folk, or traditional)
Objective	Subjective

Does the poem so burden the symbols? I think not,
but certainly the temporal context of the poem, both
in the facts of his current state of being and in the associations revealed by his retrospective autobiography,
suggests that the symbols had a long and persistent
importance to him. Taking the poem and the *Auto-
biography* together, one can discern a synoptic contemplation of sun and moon that is revealing in relation to succeeding and earlier poems.

In his earlier work, the sun and the moon operated at
two distinct yet interpenetrated levels. They were sexual symbols, and they were signs of large cosmic design.
In "Under the Moon" he used the structure of the

Ptolemaic system as it was understood in the late classical period:

> Here on the earth we are the sport of Fate; nay, on the earth itself we are worse off still. We are beneath the Moon, and beneath the moon there is not only Fate but something more unworthy and equally malignant, Chance—to say nothing of damp and the ills of earth and bad daemons.[48]

The Land-under-Wave is seen as parallel to the cosmic structure of the visible world, with sun, moon, and stars, but the lives of the gods are shaped from a blending of sun and moon rather than from their divorce:

> Land-under-Wave, where out of the moon's light and the sun's
> Seven old sisters wind the threads of the long-lived ones. . . .[49]

At the poem's close the moon appears as a rather conventional sign of the impermanence of all beauty, so that in the one poem three different meanings are assigned to the one symbol:

> Because of something told under the famished horn
> Of the hunter's moon, that hung between the night and the day,
> To dream of women whose beauty was folded in dismay,
> Even in an old story, is a burden not to be borne.

But the sun and moon are seen as forces affecting the conduct and pleasures of men, as entities of cosmic weight and intimate effect.

In other contexts, the sun and moon are listed with the stars as symbols of a rigid natural order:

> . . . you would murmur tender words,
> Forgiving me, because you were dead:
> Nor would you rise and hasten away,
> Though you have the will of the wild birds,
> But know your hair was bound and wound
> About the stars and moon and sun. . . .[50]

She would, in other words, realize and accept her limited position in the universal order. In another poem of the same date (*ca.* 1899), the heavenly bodies symbolize the order of the created world, and when the poet longs for the end of the world, he longs specifically for their disappearance:

I would that the Boar without bristles had come from the West
And had rooted the sun and moon and stars out of the sky
And lay in the darkness, grunting, and turning to his rest.[51]

The point is not merely that sun and moon and stars establish the conditions of earthly life but that the sun and moon generate universal life, of which the stars are the convenient and inclusive sign. The return to darkness is, in effect, the return to God, as Martin Hearne argues in the much revised play *The Unicorn from the Stars* (1904–1911):

We must put out the whole world as I put out this candle. We must put out the light of the stars and the light of the sun and the light of the moon, till we have brought everything to nothing once again. I saw in a broken vision, but now all is clear to me. Where there is nothing, where there is nothing—there is God! [52]

This statement has its rationale in occult thought, and Yeats himself furnishes an explication of it in his comments on Blake:

The mood of the seer, no longer bound in by the particular experiences of his body, spreads out and enters into the particular experiences of an ever-widening circle of other lives and beings, for it will more and more grow one with that portion of the mood essences which is common to all that lives. The circle of individuality will widen out until other individualities are contained within it, and their thoughts, and the persistent thought-symbols which are their spiritual or mental bodies, will grow visible to it. He who has thus passed into the impersonal portion of his own mind perceives that it is not a mind but all minds. Hence Blake's statement that "Albion," or man, once contained all "the starry heavens," and his description of their flight from him as he materialized. When once a man has re-entered into this, his ancient state, he perceives all things as with the eyes of God.[53]

He sees, in fact, what is to human eyes nothing. He returns to the primal unity before the bifurcation of God into the Sun and Moon resulted in the stars, the earth, and all that goes with it. The destructive impulse of Martin in *The Unicorn from the Stars* is, in the final analysis, identical to the creative impulse of Yeats in "Lines Written in Dejection"; both move toward the return to God, or to the God-like in man, Martin annihilating all distinctions through the simple strategy of utter destruction, Yeats reëstablishing unity through the prayerful methodology of art. Art and death, creation and destruction, are thus identified. In both instances the key symbols of disunity and struggle are the sun and the moon. The single attempt is to make distinctions meaningless by balance or by total obliteration, which would, in effect, result in balance. The destructive resolution, although it may have originated more in impatience than in deliberate choice, remained a constant concern of Yeats throughout his life, and the very violence of the intended resolution indicates how great a problem was masked and treated in Yeats's employment of the symbols.

In addition to this extensive use of the symbols to suggest cosmic and metaphysical process, he frequently used them to represent the male and female in sexual

relations. In "The Rose of Battle" (1892) Yeats in-
voked the "sad, the lonely, the insatiable," including
those who suffered from a desire for more than is "in
rain or dew / Or in the sun and moon, or on the
earth." [54] Since the argument of the poem is to flee all
temporal bounds, the sun and moon here probably sig-
nify the limits of natural love. By 1899 and "Into the
Twilight" sexual satisfaction is identified with a vague
mystical beatitude; the poem urges the "heart" to transcend the limits of judgment and division and attain
happiness in a country where the "mystical brother-
hood / Of sun and moon and hollow and wood / And
river and stream work out their will." [55] The *summum
bonum* is symbolized in alchemical and covertly sexual
terms.

In "The Song of Wandering Aengus" (1899), the
sun and moon exhibit clearly the formal balance of
cabalistic and alchemical lore and play upon the basic
meanings, the masculine and feminine, which Hermes
assigned to them. Aengus catches a "silver trout," but
when he builds up his fire to cook it, the moon-colored
trout becomes "a glimmering girl" and fades away after
calling his name and luring him after her. Aengus says
that he has not given up his chase through "hollow
lands and hilly lands" and that he will keep it up until
he rediscovers her:

> I will find out where she has gone,
> And kiss her lips and take her hands;
> And walk among long dappled grass,
> And pluck till time and times are done
> The silver apples of the moon,
> The golden apples of the sun. [56]

The apples of sun and moon are thus associated with an indolently pleasant sexual relation. The position of the two is analogous to the brief balance described by Cuchulain in *On Baile's Strand* (1903):

> I have never known love but as a kiss
> In the mid-battle, and a difficult truce
> Of oil and water, candles and dark night,
> Hillside and hollow, the hot-footed sun
> And the cold, sliding, slippery-footed moon—
> A brief forgiveness between opposites
> That have been hatreds for three times the age
> Of this long-'stablished ground.[57]

These associations work at their simplest level (sun–moon equals masculine–feminine) in numerous other poems as in *The Green Helmet* (1911), when Emer says that she is moon to Cuchulain's sun, or in "The Ragged Wood" (1903), in which the sun and moon are directly presented as lovers. In "Under the Round Tower" (1918?) the antithetical pair are treated humorously, while retaining a simple reference to their masculine–feminine meaning. A beggar, unable to find other shelter, decides to pass the night on "great-grandfather's battered tomb," but when he lies down to sleep, he dreams of the sun and moon bellowing and prancing for an hour. The "golden king and silver lady" prance up the typically Yeatsean spiral stair of a tower until they have attained the top and mastery of both mind and body sufficient to allow sweetness in dance and song. And there they stay:

> That golden king and that wild lady
> Sang till stars began to fade,
> Hands gripped in hands, toes close together,

Hair spread on the wind they made;
That lady and that golden king
Could like a brace of blackbirds sing.

The vision is wasted on the rambling jailbird, who decides to pick a pocket and rent a bed in some other locale:

"I cannot find the peace of home
On great-grandfather's battered tomb." [58]

Against such a background, even the conventional uses of the moon, its appearance when waning as a symbol of unhappy or thwarted love ("Adam's Curse," 1903) or when full as a symbol of successful love ("A Memory of Youth," 1914), are intelligibly enriched by the basic sexual associations. For if male and female are to be symbolized by sun and moon, then the full moon, the complete illumination, sun in moon and moon in sun, is a reasonable symbol for the solved antinomy of both sex and nature.

These occurrences of the sun and moon predate *A Vision* and are in many ways similar to the symbolic habits already explored with reference to the swan—the tendency toward allegory, the deliberate checking of that tendency by the intervention of associations not necessarily compatible with the fixed reference to a pre-structured symbology, the movement from philosophical to literary tradition, from the cabala to romantic convention, from evocation to notation. Dramatic context further shapes these variant meanings, so that in "Lines Written in Dejection" Yeats convoked a host of associations that integrated life with dream. This poem is a focal point that, while not in itself characteristic (so

much convocation being impossible with any frequency), dramatizes the sense of fruitfully intersecting
life and dream, person and superhuman, that was his
constant preoccupation. The dream and its associations
led to icons central not only to this single poem but to
"Two Songs from a Play" and "On a Picture of a Black
Centaur." The biographical confusions surrounding this
latter poem, the question of whether the black centaur
was in a picture by Dulac or one by Salkeld, may come
from the fact that any later picture merely triggered the
response already stored from this dream:

> There is a fragment of a very early Greek pot showing two
> roughly drawn centaurs with long thin legs, one of the centaurs
> touching with his hand a tree which has long leaves and what
> seems to be a round fruit. Above the centaurs, but apparently
> separate from the tree a bird perches.[59]

His deliberately extensive record of this dream implies
that his use of icons often came from a similar design,
that is, a habit of tracing associations out to their furthest
extremities so that they led to still new centers of association, his personal reminiscence of this particular dream
leading to a reconstruction of its discerned associations.
He then noted the bearing of the sun and moon in systems of folklore and religion and followed them on to
further associations with yet other systems, the chain
breaking at certain points to allow him to move into a
freer and wider exploration.

The associations built through three decades of intensive contemplation and poetic use were not cast aside
because of the sudden intervention of the symbology of
A Vision, and this fact alone should make one suspicious
of the ultimate efficacy of that book in the resolution

of difficulties in Yeats's later poems. There is a sense in which *A Vision* can best be considered as a self-integrated and complete poetic structure rather than as a storehouse of images for poetry, and Yeats's persistent playing on associations with the sun and moon that are at most obliquely related to those in *A Vision* suggests a wider set of origins for the key heavenly icons than one book.

When in "The Tower," for instance, the young men mistake "the brightness of the moon / For the prosaic light of day," the associations are similar to those of "Lines Written in Dejection," the moon being associated with the imagination, and with delusive and bewitching feminine beauty. And when in the same poem the speaker prays for artistic triumph he asks for the blending of sun and moon that formed the life of the gods and the art of men:

> O may the moon and sunlight seem
> One inextricable beam,
> For if I triumph I must make men mad.[60]

The defeat of reason is the defeat of the sun, "And if that memory recur, the sun's / Under eclipse and the day blotted out." When he thinks of the totality he sees the same triad that Martin Hearne had wished to destroy and that the boar without bristles was to root out of the sky:

> Death and life were not
> Till man made up the whole,
> Made lock, stock and barrel
> Out of his bitter soul,
> Aye, sun and moon and star, all. . . .[61]

In this one poem the moon is used to suggest the fall from unity into diversity, the imagination, feminine enchantment, and one of the antithetical forces that compose art.

This poem was completed in 1925, and like many of the poems written after 1917 it plays on meanings already established in Yeats's early poetry. In "Nineteen Hundred and Nineteen," for instance, the moon is the sign of the disorderly rule to which men and their artifacts are subject: ". . . the circle of the moon / That pitches common things about." In the same poem the sun was the rational force of the legislative intellect: ". . . habits that made old wrong / Melt down, as it were wax in the sun's rays. . . ." [62] The association of the moon with beauty and feminine coldness that Cuchulain had expressed in *The Green Helmet* appeared again in "First Love," "Human Dignity," and other poems in the sequence *A Man Young and Old*. And in "All Souls' Night" the classical sense of the moon as a symbol of sublunary disorder and limitation, already noted in "Nineteen Hundred and Nineteen," is contrasted with the sun surprisingly used as a repository of all value. The sun and moon appear together as the signs of generated life in "Vacillation," and in "Those Dancing Days are Gone" (*"I carry the sun in a golden cup, / The moon in a silver bag."*) [63] he reverts to the very early associations exploited in "The Song of Wandering Aengus." When in "Parting," that lovely aubade, the woman attempts to hold the man from flight, she answers his fear that "Daylight already flies / From mountain crest to crest" with the perfectly conventional response, "That light is from the moon," [64] and whatever force this statement gains from the associations with the icon in other poems, its chief power here comes out of the established dramatic convention in which the poem lives. In "He and She," the sexual connotations of the two icons are the clear simple base of their use.

In large part these icons in the later poetry repeat, extend, and provide new contexts for the associations convoked during Yeats's 1915 reminiscences. The difference between these uses and those properly associated with *A Vision* comes from the fact that in *A Vision* he deliberately suppresses one term—the sun—of the antinomies represented by sun and moon. The moon in solitude becomes the sign of generative force, and the dark of the moon gathers to itself the complex of meaning otherwise associated with the sun, the objectivity, the masculinity. With the sun suppressed, he uses other icons—the hawk in "Meditations in Time of Civil War," the rough beast of "The Second Coming," the tower of "Blood and the Moon"—to contrast with the full moon of subjective attainment. The extremes of possibility are then symbolized by the full or the dark of the moon, and these extremes are localized in historical eras.

In "Byzantium," for example, the opening stanza presents as alternates of possibility either moon- or starlight, in early drafts [65] ". . . a silence lit / Whether by star or moon . . ." or the protagonist looks on the town "Under the starlight dome . . ." as he wanders the town's intricacies. Finally Yeats made the formulation "A starlit or a moonlit dome distains / All that man is . . . ," and he insisted on the spelling of *distains* to his editor in the interests of the pun on superiority and purification. It was a purity opposed to the intricacies and complexities of the "aimless flood of imagery," the "bleak complexity" and "bitter furies" rising from "That dolphin-torn, that gong-tormented sea." It does not much matter whether the "dome" refers to the heavenly dome of the skies or the dome of Santa Sophia or, as is likely, both, the main point being that merely human life is impossible at the dark (starlight) or full (moonlight) of the moon, and that human life attains purity and death at those points (it is distained).

What does matter in the reading of this crucial stanza is the question of whether it refers to the dome as purely an aesthetic object: any artifact, no matter how it is lit, is superior to and stands for purification of human complexity; or as sign of an absolute condition: the dome of the sky or that dome as reflected in the dome of this glorious artifact is superior to and capable of purging human impurities to the extent that it approaches an absolute condition, that is, full moon or dark. The question is also central to the reading of "Blood and the Moon," which is in like manner concerned with the relation between the fury and mire of human veins and the absolute purity of the moon. The initial phrasing of the lines in "Byzantium" suggests that the quality of light rather than architecture is the chief point (". . . a silence lit / Whether by star or moon . . ."), and this is reinforced by the fact that the poem's protagonist looks on the town "Under the starlight dome . . ." as he wanders the mazes of the town. And the manuscripts of "Blood and the Moon," as well as the finished poem, suggest the same ascription of absolute quality to the moon:

> Though all the land impure, the purity of the moon
> Falls along the narrow loop hole to the passage floor

In the final printed version, these lines read:

> The purity of the unclouded moon
> Has flung its arrowy shaft upon the floor

And he refers, in the manuscripts, to the moon as "That purity" and "That pale purity." [66]

This final use of the moon as inclusive sign of purity and power, which prevails in *The Winding Stair*, is a dominant possibility in the poems from 1917 to 1933. The uses of the moon in *Last Poems* are surprisingly remote from the various preoccupations so far discussed. When he urges Dorothy Wellesley to "Stretch towards the moonless midnight of the trees," the moonlessness is simple lightlessness and mystery, that dark from which emerge the great terrors of existence, rather than any reference to the associations so far examined. In the third of the three marching songs, when the old man takes down the moon to rattle out a tune, it is simply an extravagant hyperbolic gesture, with no implications of purity, innocence, femininity, imagination, and so on. Except for these two examples, the sun and the moon are as absent in these supposedly "summary" poems as is the swan. There is a great deal of treatment of light and dark, but the heavenly bodies are hardly mentioned.

What we are to make of this I will discuss in the following section. But it seems to me extremely revealing that Yeats should have—how could it be less than deliberately?—suppressed these icons that, in the period from 1917 to 1933, he had considered central to the qualities of his verse, emblematic of his nature and motives. The poems we know as *Last Poems* were looked on by Yeats as *New Poems,* and so when half of them were printed as a volume during his life he titled them.

Last Uses

Yeats treated his obsessive icons as he treated the special members of his spiritual coven, Lady Gregory, Maud Gonne, Crazy Jane, Cuchulain: they were his centers where values were visible. They aroused emotion, suggested fresh passionate foci, but were sufficiently complex to remain mysterious and powerful beyond any fixed meaning. In *Last Poems* the chief participants in his spiritual drama, whether particular persons or imagined figures, were frequently convoked to justify or illuminate his life. They were contemplated, questioned, judged, and in one striking poem, discarded. The testamentary motives already explored in *The Tower* again took powerful place in his verse, and as he moved toward death he sought new figures that would support his permanent life (for example, Dorothy Wellesley) and looked in the records of history and art both for vindication of his past conduct and support in the weakness and solitude of his present condition. In like manner, many of his habitual icons were convoked, most patently in "The Gyres," a poem that gets a great deal of its force from echoes of preceding works and that has the tone of admitting the reader to conspiratorial intimacy. He treats his earlier verse as a recognizable body of classical literature to which he can allude with free confidence. The gyres themselves are central to the symbology of *A Vision* and related poems, and the similarities between passages in "The Gyres" and other poems are more than the casual parallels inevitable in any poet's work:

> For beauty dies of beauty, worth of worth. . . .
> ("The Gyres") [67]

> Love's pleasure drives his love away,
> The painter's brush consumes his dreams. . . .
> ("Two Songs from a Play") [68]

When he speaks of the "irrational streams of blood" that are staining earth, he evokes the "blood-dimmed tide" of "The Second Coming." The "numb nightmare" parallels the "nightmare" of "Nineteen Hundred and Nineteen," and the "blood and mire" is a play on the "mire or blood" of "Byzantium." "The Gyres" takes much of its authority from its reference to preceding texts and has some of the quality of mosaic self-pastiche.

It is not surprising to see this quality in what were to be the last poems of a man who had devoted a great part of his life to meditation upon a set of related icons. What is surprising is that this last book should suppress the very natural impulse to summarize and exploit what had already been realized under original creative pressure. My own suspicion is that a poem like "The Gyres" is a prayerlike effort to keep open the channels of creativity, to maintain the habit of composition. "The Gyres" does iconographically what "The Municipal Gallery Revisited" does dramatically; that is, it plays upon previously established associations. Instead of creating contexts that release meaning, it certifies meanings already habitual: in the body of Yeats's verse it is merely conventional, playing upon agreements already established with the audience. The "sense of quotation" that it evokes is like the special pedantry of Eliot, except that the tradition used is what Yeats called "the tradition of myself." It seems to me an example of the egotism that Yeats disliked, for it depends upon a kind of characterization of the speaker. Readers already familiar with the poetry have their habits gratified, and those coming to the poem as an early experience with Yeats are invited and often seduced to become participants in those habits.

The violence of "The Gyres" is one characteristic of the *Last Poems* that puzzles and repels readers, and the tone is by no means assignable to the violent subject matter thrust upon him by a world plainly on its way to the holocaust of World War II: the tone comes from the attitude, and this in turn derives from the personal dramatic situation in which he finds himself. The most direct indication of his sense of circumstance appears in "An Acre of Grass":

> Picture and book remain,
> An acre of green grass
> For air and exercise,
> Now strength of body goes;
> Midnight, an old house
> Where nothing stirs but a mouse.
>
> My temptation is quiet.
> Here at life's end
> Neither loose imagination,
> Nor the mill of the mind
> Consuming its rag and bone,
> Can make the truth known.

Grant me an old man's frenzy,
Myself must I remake
Till I am Timon and Lear
Or that William Blake
Who beat upon the wall
Till truth obeyed his call;

A mind Michael Angelo knew
That can pierce the clouds,
Or inspired by frenzy
Shake the dead in their shrouds;
Forgotten else by mankind,
An old man's eagle mind.[69]

With fresh experience no longer easily available to him, he still could turn to works of visual and literary art, and he could take pleasure in the enclosed cultivated garden. These were permanent and reparable, while the decay of the body was not reversible. Within this civilized complex, he presented his overriding psychological and spiritual problems in terms at once general and self-derisive. The scarecrow, the battered kettle tied to a dog's heel—these are predecessors (in *The Tower*) of the rag and bone shop of the heart of this poem and "The Circus Animals' Desertion." These decrepitudes in turn were paralleled by threats to the artifacts of an equally dying social order. What preserved those artifacts was the passion they embodied from the past and the power they might liberate in the present, and this passion was the restorative dramatic force of figures acting out their proper universal role. Old age heightened the threatful power of natural and historical processes moving toward death. The regret of "An Acre of Grass" denies the legitimacy of the "temptation" to remain placidly content with picture and book—even his own book—and the confined garden. The poem drives first toward the subjective decay of the body and finally toward a renewed vigor in the quest for truth. It leaves behind the habitual conditions of safety, at least in assertion, and in so doing displays a tension between the habits of his poetic activity and a desire to break free.

The freedom invited and feared is the freedom from life that only death provides. T. S. Eliot suggests that the *Last Poems* express the plight of old age without any hope of salvation,[70] but in so arguing he is insisting on orthodoxy to an extent that unfairly damages the poems. The tone of restlessness, discontent, dissatisfaction that characterizes the book comes from a disappointment with experience and a reluctance to leave the chance of novel revelation. But the ultimate revelation of death is looked on with distaste because of its uselessness. He cannot be absolute for life or death, and the joy that he proposes as fitting to tragic figures at the point of death is charged with a strained pressure. The "hysterical women" of "Lapis Lazuli" were perfectly right, and although Yeats is also right in asserting that not even a producer of drama could be so foolish as to have Cleopatra weep at her approaching doom, he is confusing life with spectacle. So long as tragic doom can be placed against a backdrop, it is not human but theatrical, and the weakness of Yeats's dramatic view of the world is that it offers temptations of melodrama. In these poems the thirst for experience is mingled with an intense dislike for the experience that the actual historical process presents to him, so that

his romantic desire for subject matter turns to disgust
as he contemplates the ugliness of his body and the
disintegration of the social order that he had been ele-
gizing for over thirty years. Against that background he
sees his accomplishment and current predicament. One
result was the remarkable poem "The Circus Animals'
Desertion," which at early stages of composition had
for title first "Despair" and then "On the Lack of a
Theme." In one early draft, after enumerating several
of his early themes, it closed with an especially revealing stanza:

> O hour of triumph come and make me gay!
> If burnished chariots are put to flight
> Why brood upon old triumph, prepare to die;
> Even at the approach of the un-imaged night
> Man has the refuge of his gaiety;
> A dab of black enhances every white,
> Tension is but the vigour of the mind,
> Cannon the god and father of mankind.[71]

The frustration, consequent violence, and ultimate wel-
coming of biological death and social destruction
("Bring war in our time, O Lord . . .") that appear in
this renounced stanza are evident in several of the
Last Poems. Death is the hour of triumph; violence the
rightful ruler of the world; tension is not only the condition of being but its controller. Mere energy in itself
seems to be enough, with no qualitative discriminations made. Gaiety does not here transfigure "all that
dread" as it did in "Lapis Lazuli" but serves as an
evasion and hiding place. The stanza was rejected, and
in its place he wrote a stanza on the lowly origins of the

splendid chariots and turned his mind to the "sweep-
ings of the street":

> Those masterful images because complete
> Grew in pure mind, but out of what began?
> A mound of refuse or the sweepings of a street,
> Old kettles, old bottles, and a broken can,
> Old iron, old bones, old rags, that raving slut
> Who keeps the till. Now that my ladder's gone,
> I must lie down where all the ladders start,
> In the foul rag-and-bone shop of the heart.[72]

Both stanzas deal with the end of experience and the
end of "masterful images," on which the first part of
the poem had dwelt and relied.

Certainly the rejected stanza was not close to Yeats's
heart, and the carelessness of the writing ("A dab of
black enhances every white . . .") shows a superficial-
ity of perception that could come only from weariness
and neglect. It serves several purposes, however, for
any one considering the ultimate phase of Yeats's iconography. It makes explicit the attitudes of the *Last
Poems,* the frustration, the impatience, the tendency
toward a destructive resolution of problems, and the
espousal of attitudes that deny the efficacy of rational
and humane measures. The personal battleground then
is projected upon the social scene. Comparing this
stanza with the poems of his middle years on the same
subject ("All Things Can Tempt Me," "A Coat"), I
find that the chief difference is that the earlier poems
closed with the psychological and aesthetic implications of his condition, as did the final version of "The
Circus Animals' Desertion." But whether he converted

the personal symptom into a public symbol or simply declared his psychological state, the basic frame of mind of *Last Poems* was constant, that is, frenzied.

And it is here that the *Last Poems* are most revealing, for they are not poems exploring with a sense of fresh insight certain themes and icons and personae that come obsessively to the poet's attention. They are, on the one hand, restatements and, on the other, explicit or implicit denials. Their basic subject is the inadequacy of habit to his current situation, and the habits are his poetic as well as his personal designs.

What is striking in the iconography of this final book is the evaluation of his earlier uses, not the mere summary or continuation. What appears to be summary is in effect a negation, for in poems like "The Gyres" a door is closed on the chance that the icons can reveal fresh possibilities: the contexts are by now defined and fixed. To return to the icons of the swan and of the sun and moon, the latter pair entered Yeats's mind when he was working on the early versions of "The Statues," as they frequently did during the later period of his writing. The brevity of their appearance suggests that they could not be relied on to carry the poem, so that Buddha's knowledge of "What drives the sun and moon" became his certainty that "Mirror on mirror mirrored is all the show." This rejection figures in little the larger rejections of *Last Poems*.

Yeats's dissatisfaction with his work was constitutional, and it is entirely fitting that discontent should be the major tone of his last poems. He took some pleasure in publicly admitting that Ezra Pound had returned the manuscript of the lyrics from *A Full Moon in March* with the single word "Putrid" scrawled on it, but in the privacy of his journal he noted that Pound had charged the poems with being written in "Nobody's language," and he then went about the task of systematically re-writing the poems, some in prose first so that he could get closer to normal language.[73] And yet another story shows that Pound was not always merely impudent in treating the work of his aging master, for when he and Yeats were in London in 1938 he told Yeats that he liked some of his new poems very much. This may have been a simple courtesy offered to his friend as he moved to-ward death, but Yeats was deeply moved by it. I suspect that Pound saw in the poems of Yeats's last months a genuine effort to break free, a persistent drive toward an idiom that would allow him to keep from merely repeating his already richly elaborated set of icons. Much of the framework of Yeats's iconographic habits remained, the contrast between light and dark, the re-liance on the force of artifacts, whether statues or paintings, the use of the imagery of sea, dolphin, tower, tree, blood and bone, all these were informing factors in the shape of many of the poems. But the tone of the last poems leaves the book free of any pretense of finality, of peaceful security. A deeper exploration of the centered and established was not the motive, and in the place of measured and knowledgeable contempla-tion the book puts a discontented denial and a furious drive toward new revelation, both of these seen against the impending term to experience.

I cannot believe that anyone is really satisfied with what is often taken as Yeats's summary statement, "Under Ben Bulben." The blunt epitaph is almost as

eloquent on the page as *in situ,* and it expresses not
the summation of a career but the tone of his closing
months:

> Cast a cold eye
> On life, on death.
> Horseman, pass by! [74]

The balance of life and death implies the impossibility
of commitment to either, and the tragedy of Yeats's last
years lay in the inevitable failure of any commitment.
He could not rest content in any achievement, and he
was forced to cast serious doubt on the accomplishments of his life. He could not trust for support his
dying friends, his dying civilization, or his own diminishing energies. What opened before him had no re-
deeming solution and what stretched behind him was
irrelevant. His exultation could come in accepting his
role out of joy rather than duty or habit, and his tragedy
came when he saw his role outworn:

> When a man grows old his joy
> Grows more deep day after day,
> His empty heart is full at length,
> But he has need of all that strength
> Because of the increasing Night
> That opens her mystery and fright.
> *Fifteen apparitions have I seen;*
> *The worst a coat upon a coat-hanger.*[75]

The *Last Poems* cannot be taken as an outcome of
Yeats's career in the sense that they are the end toward
which he was moving. In the hesitations, the pauses and
occasional plunges that he took in his poetry, there was
always a residue of motive that allowed him to move
onward to yet another attack on the problems that he

had elected as his. Rather than carry on the processes of immediately preceding poems, the *Last Poems* are in method and tone much closer to the poems of *Responsibilities* and *The Wild Swans at Coole* in their effortful groping toward some mode of being that would liberate him. Hence *The Tower* is more vividly successful as a testamentary volume, for there he is contemplating and exploiting the possibilities of a defined and accepted idiom and iconography. There is no air of experiment in it, as there is in *Last Poems,* and there is no genuine displeasure in considering the poetic means at his disposal. So in the *Last Poems* he returns to the ballads of his earlier verse, strips his life of its pretenses, attempts to reach again the foundation of his poetic action, and denies the temptation of merely exploiting his established iconography. It was not in Yeats's habit of being possible to be summary and dismissive:

> While man can still his body keep
> Wine or love drug him to sleep,
> Waking he thanks the Lord that he
> Has body and its stupidity,
> But body gone he sleeps no more,
> And till his intellect grows sure
> That all's arranged in one clear view,
> Pursues the thoughts that I pursue,
> Then stands in judgment on his soul,
> And, all work done, dismisses all
> Out of intellect and sight
> And sinks at last into the night.[76]

And after defining this last arrangement, he concludes the poem by returning to the distractions of suffering life. The desire for the final statement was present but always doubted, and he could no more rely on his iconography than on his personality to carry the entire burden. Ultimate reality can be "symbolized but not known," and a placid resting in any given set of symbols would imply knowledge allegorical in fullness. His attitudes toward iconography and dramaturgy were equally restless, and in his final iconography as in his final dramaturgy he held to the principles of his very last letter, in which he expressed his wish to write his most fundamental thought so that he could in effect dismiss all. He was happy in the prospect:

> It seems to me that I have found what I wanted. When I try to put it all into a phrase I say, 'Man can embody truth but he cannot know it.' I must embody it in the completion of my life. The abstract is not life and everywhere draws out its contradictions. You can refute Hegel but not the Saint or the Song of Sixpence. . . .[77]

The final form could never appear.

the passionate syntax

In poetry, every word matters.

Iɴ the composition of Yeats's poems, the linear structures controlled the movement of the language in a flexible, ordered pattern that worked on principles that disciplined his passionate syntax and permitted free variations in accord with the vocalic emergencies of his speech. His concern with a passionate syntax he expressed frequently, and, as he remarked in his later years, the varied rhythmic forms of his plays came from a desire to achieve completeness of range. Prosody had within it an implied life, and what he saw in blank verse was a life that he associated with the isolation of person from person which resulted in a loss of "that ancient Self" in favor of the individual intellect. His intervention of song patterns within the

181

blank verse structure meant that he could bring into his work ". . . a ghostly voice, an unvariable possibility, an unconscious norm"[1] which invigorated and gave universality to the otherwise divisive blank verse line. This range from individuated speech to embodied passion was the range of his dramaturgy and iconography, and it was matched by his prosody.

The aim of his verse was wholeness of being, the incorporation in art of life seen at its fullest and most healing. In his long poems, "Vacillation" or "Nineteen Hundred and Nineteen," his dramatic and iconographic variety was matched by a prosody that could speak in the elaborate civilized form of decasyllabic lines in ottava rima with as much ease as it expressed generalized emotion in lines measured by stress, so that their dramatic structure would admit the entire possibility of experience. And his books of poems showed the same kind of fullness, evident in the adaptations of ballad meter in "Crazy Jane and Jack the Journeyman" and the meditative formal speech of "Coole Park and Ballylee, 1931."

His general aim was to present experience with fullness and precision. He had in mind a wide variety of possible verbal relations or schema, acceptable movements of words that he entertained as possible modes of accommodating experience. Working on a poem, he would begin under pressure from almost any source, his reading in history or philosophy, the events of daily life, his experience with artifacts. He would then seek out the proper rhythmic form, and, once his sense of the appropriate line was established, he would work within those limits, refining and heightening his syntax always in collaboration with the demands of stanzaic form. He had a few private conventions, for instance his attempt to make period and stanza coincide, but generally he worked within a fairly stable and rational prosody. If he were writing a brief intense lyric, he tended toward designs that fell into a pattern of a fixed number of major stresses per line. If he were engaged in a reflective and meditative poem of some intellectual complexity with didactic tone, he would tend toward the decasyllabic line and a stanza that at once curtailed and gave sufficient room for the development of concept and icon. Under the weight of his passionate syntax, the line would sometimes break the frame of stress or syllabic count, but his long association with the movement of the line provided him with a set of compensations that allowed for divergence without destroying the felt linear unity of the poem.

I extrapolate these general ideas from a variety of sources, his published and unpublished notes on prosody, his much-marked copy of Thomas Mac-Donagh's book on Anglo-Irish poetry, and the manuscript and printed versions of the poems. Yeats's own overt comments on prosody are seldom detailed; he gives away few secrets, even when discussing his early experiments with Florence Farr on speaking to the psaltery. Except for brief notes on poetry and music, his statements on prosody tend to be exalted and rhapsodic in tone. Witnesses to his informal remarks and close acquaintances have made conflicting comments on his rhythmic sense. He composed to a tune, but he was tone-deaf. He spoke his verse in a monotonous chant, but his capacity for detecting minutiae of enunciation in the readings of others outran description. He counted syllables in shaping his lines but sometimes got confused and came up with hypermetric lines; and at the same time, he was a master of verse. He loved the idea of having his poems sung, but he hated musicians. He wrote plays all his life, but he hated actors. He knew nothing about scansion, but everything about versification. He liked to think of his metrical ability as mysterious and instinctive in origin, and in a letter to Edith Shackleton Heald, written in 1937, he displayed at once his care in metrical matters and his steady insistence on his ignorance of them:

> . . . When you read this last poem ["Those Images"] of mine, be careful to get the scansion of the third line of the second stanza right. There must be an accent on 'from'—'Turn from drudgery'—You will notice how bothered I am when I get to prosody—because it is the most certain of my instincts, it is the subject of which I am most ignorant. I do not even know if I should write the mark of accent or stress thus \ or thus /. . . .[2]

The line in question was abandoned before the poem saw print, but his marking of it exhibits his concern with a stress prosody that would express most clearly his sense of the vocalic pressure behind any poetic statement.

There are, in unpublished as well as published material, many indications of his deep concern with the relation between speech, song, and poetry, and in the process he ranges widely over the history of English verse. I quote one passage at length because it is unknown and especially revealing:

> I have been wondering why I like a lyric that sings, rather than talks, to go to an old rhythm, to sound as if men might sing it when half asleep, or when riding on a journey. Today for the

first time after months of wondering I have hit it. If a poem talks, a good sonnet (say Blunt's that begins "When I heard laughing at the tavern door") we have the passionate syntax, the impression of the man who speaks, the active man no abstract poet, the drama; but if it sings we want the impression of a man either actually singing, or at least murmuring it over, and not as a show, a performance, but at some moment of emotion. We cannot do this if the poem does not call up the image of sailors, of horsemen or unhappy lovers, a multitude out of other days. I want . . . when I cannot get the syntax of common passionate life (and I seldom can in a song), a measure that seems a part of that life. The second part of Burns' Mathew [*sic*] Henderson has such a measure, and Lionel Johnson's poem that sings [rings?] on "What are the winds and what are the waters, near are your eyes." That poem is a perfect speech indeed but it is still more a perfect song. The Blunt poem is a speech only. "Golden Numbers" is all song.

Tennyson's syntax is seldom contorted . . . it is perhaps never good speech. It lacks the impulse of passionate life. "In Memoriam" is detestable because of its syntax.

Browning wrote speech not passionate speech. He wrote a language which he studied from outside as if it were a dialect, and he got his impression of reality from ejaculations and suppressions, which are all an avoidance of the expression of passion. Only at rare moments do we get a passionate rhythmical syntax, and often when he is most poetic as in that song about the "aloe balls" in Paracelsus he is furthest from the natural order of words.

We tolerate, or enjoy an artificial syntax and a rhythm that is neither speech, nor anything suggesting a song because our thought is artificial. Milton began it by bringing into English Literature a mass of thought "to justify the ways of God" when it was believed to have value apart from its value as dramatization. In Dante when he is not dramatizing [,?] some lost or suffering soul gives us an emotion of passionate ecstacy. His Paradiso is a mystic vision, an exaltation. He writes it all for that ecstacy's sake, not for the edification of others. Milton brought the mischief from Rome which systematized what had been natural impulse in Greece, and he thought more of the state than of Paradise, and in Dryden and Pope the mischief is there unmixed—sheer dry lies. Burns and Blake are a revolt, but Wordsworth and even Coleridge and Shelley in much of their work follow Dryden and Milton. So too did Tennyson. The exact equivalent of this tradition in poetry was the academic form of the painter and sculptor. . . .

The revolt against impersonal eloquence climaxed at the end of the last century and that against impersonal form at the beginning of this. In painting, observed form was substituted, characterization took the place of beauty. Browning to some extent did the like in poetry but there it is wrong because character cannot be made subject to beauty, which is passion. Character is the obstruction of passion. . . . in Burns, in Verlaine and in "the poets of the 90's" there was disorder of life and in Blake a violence of opinion resultant from the rebellion against that traditional eloquence, with its classical morality. Blake alone saw that it was classical not christian morality in origin. It is christian now because it no longer derives itself from its old pride—lonely to the lone I come divine to the divinity—but is imposed by "the sense of duty," duty that is to others.

The escape is personal expression, or drama. But this personal expression must not become characterization nor in poetry can drama itself become chiefly characterization. In personal expression characterization is egotism.[3]

This is a long sequence of rumination, the last paragraph of which I have already quoted in the first chapter, but it is revealing in the same way that one of his diaries is which began with the portentous title "Diary of Thought" but after three meditative pages suddenly opened out into a sequence of poems on death. In Yeats's mind the movement from questions of prosody and syntax to excursions into literary, artistic, and religious history, and thence back to prosody, was natural and inevitable.

The specific statements on syntax and poetry in this passage are characteristic of his preoccupations. The division between speech and song that this passage discusses is the chief division of his work, and it is also the chief division of his prosody. In his meditative speeches, his dramatic attempts to project a persona, now more, now less directly related to his circumstantial daily character, his sense of the line tended to stay within the limits of syllabic measure; that is, his lines were not pentameter but decasyllabic in intent. In his songs, his attempts to speak out of an impersonal depth of primitive feeling, the line tended to be measured by stresses, so that a three-stress line might have as few as three and as many as seven syllables. The line cited in his letter to Edith Heald is a case in point:

Turn from drudgery

He did not retain the line, but it does indicate his concern with stress that is perhaps even more clear in the extremely beautiful short poem "Her Anxiety":

Earth in beauty dressed
Awaits returning spring.
All true love must die,
Alter at the best
Into some lesser thing.
Prove that I lie.

Such body lovers have,
Such exacting breath,
That they touch or sigh.
Every touch they give,

Lóve is neárer déath.
Próve thát I líe.[4]

It would be possible to say that the poem is basically
iambic, that eight of the ten lines in the body of the
poem begin with a headless iamb and the refrain is
anomalous and a law to itself. Well, no: each line has
three heavy stresses, including the refrain, which Yeats
wanted to have read (according to his manuscript
markings)

Próve thát I líe.

Other poems using the same basic line (see the analysis of "Mohini Chatterjee" below) show even a wider
range of variation in syllable count while maintaining
the three-stress norm.

In the songs written in this stress prosody, the variation in syllable count can be remarkably wide. In the
formal speeches, the encomia on Lady Gregory and
Coole Park, the oratorical sections of "Nineteen Hundred and Nineteen," and other poems discursive, declarative, and oratorical in tone, the decasyllabic lines
are infrequently more or less than ten syllables, and
when they appear to have an extra syllable, it can easily
be explained by an elision that would take place in the
speaking of the line ("memory," for example). Within
the decasyllabic line, the intent is to load the line with
major stresses, and the fact that the variation in syllables is negligible indicates that, if Yeats *was* writing
in accentual feet, he certainly made infrequent substi-
tutions of anapest or dactyl for iamb and extremely
frequent use of the spondee. It seems to me, however,

unlikely that he used a foot prosody in view of the fact
that his manuscripts give *no* example of scanning by
feet.

In Yeats's library are two books by Thomas Mac-
Donagh on prosody, the first on *Thomas Campion and
the Art of English Poetry,* the second a series of *Studies
Irish and Anglo-Irish.*[5] The books are heavily annotated,
with pencil marks indicating important passages and a
list at the back of the second book of important pages.
Both the hand and the habit of notation indicate, as
Mrs. W. B. Yeats says, that the books were marked not
by Yeats but by Ezra Pound. It is probable that these
books were taken in the winter of 1916 to Surrey, where
Pound read to Yeats in order to spare his dimming eye-
sight. The prosodic concepts are often extremely close
to those which I have taken to be the dominant motives
of Yeats's poetry: "In speech-verse the normal line has a
fixed number of syllables. In song-verse the normal line
has a fixed number of periods, marked by accentual
beat, with fixed places for the beat to fall." [6] In discussing the difference between English and Irish verse
rhythms MacDonagh expanded on the concept of the
syllabic line:

> English rhythm is governed by stress. In England the tend-
> ency is to hammer the stressed syllables and to slur the un-
> stressed syllables. In Ireland we keep by comparison a uniform
> stress. A child in Cork, reading the word *unintelligibility,* pro-
> nounced all the eight syllables distinctly without any special
> stress on any, though his voice rises and falls in a kind of tune
> or croon, going high upon the final syllable. Early Irish verse
> is syllabic. The lines are measured by the number of syllables.
> In modern verse, both Irish and English, the lines are measured
> by the feet, and commonly the feet differ from one another in

the number of syllables: each foot has one stressed syllable. In common English verse the voice goes from stress to stress, hammering the stress. In most Anglo-Irish verse the stresses are not so strongly marked; the unstressed syllables are more fully pronounced; the whole effect is different.[7]

In line with these general ideas, he makes two analyses of Yeats's verse that, though more declarative than analytic, have a genuine cogency. He speaks first of "The Lake Isle of Innisfree," and particularly of the line "And I shall have some peace there, for peace comes dropping slow. . . ." His primary suggestion here is that the norms of utterance are the line and the phrase, indicated by a cesura:

Take the line frankly as if it were a line of prose, only with that beauty of vibration in the voice that goes with the fine grave words of poetry. (It is impossible to mark the reading by punctuation or the like.) Read it so, and you will understand the true quality of this mode in Anglo-Irish poetry. It is wrong to scan this verse, to cut off the syllables according to the measure of a rhythm that rises and falls sharply and regularly. Even with some marks to indicate that though unstressed a syllable is slow and long:

And I shall have some peace there

the scansion is wrong. There is a recurrence in this verse, but it is not a recurrence of the foot. I have been able to take half a line to illustrate my meaning. The first three lines of each stanza have a cesura in the middle. I believe that that is the only division to make in them, and that as a rule open to exception. In general the second part of the line has a more obvious recurrence of stress than the first, as

. . . of clay and wattles made.

Of course, as in all musical verse, there are contrasts. . . .[8]

For evasiveness, this series of notes ranks fairly high. It denies the possibility of any but the most general approach, and nothing could be less abashed in the advocacy of impressionism. How are we to understand ". . . that beauty of vibration in the voice that goes with the fine grave words of poetry"? And how are we to decide what constitutes fineness and graveness? Mac-Donagh was not intent, however, on answering such questions. He wanted simply to suggest a quality, and in doing so he showed something about the tune that Yeats was supposed to mumble and hum as he shaped poems. The cesural structure of "The Lake Isle" is a major prosodic tone in Yeats's poetry:

> I will aríse and gó nów
> And go to Innisfree
> And a smáll cábin buíld thére
> Of clay and wattles made [9]

> I knów althoúgh when loóks meét
> I tremble to the bone
> The móre I leáve the doór unlátched
> The sooner love is gone
> For lóve is bút a skeín unwóund
> Between the dark and dawn [10]

In both instances, we have the initial assertive statement moving to heavily bunched stresses at the close, and this to be followed by a less violent and more regularly stressed statement not of action but of quality or scene. When Yeats spoke of "Innisfree" as the first of his lyrics to have in it something of his own music, he was certainly right. The norm of this line incorporates

the qualities of traditional ballad meter and of the fourteener, which Yeats used in his play *The Green Helmet*
and in some of his lyrics. The result was a line that had
the qualities of folk song and yet the carrying force of
a very long line without its cumbersomeness. The long
line of Swinburne or Whitman was too lax for his purposes, and the tension exerted between his sophisticated
subject matter and the primitive structure of his line
gave his work a peculiar tension and distinction. The
cadence of the long line and the stress of the ballad
meter blended in a new entity.

In "Innisfree" one can detect a cadence that underlies much of Yeats's later work and rises to dominance
in "A Man Young and Old" and many poems in *Last
Poems*. In addition to his description of "Innisfree,"
MacDonagh commented on one other lyric, from the
play *Deirdre:*

First Musician

'Why is it,' Queen Edain said,
'If I do but climb the stair
To the tower overhead,
When the winds are calling there,
Or the gannets calling out
In waste spaces of the sky,
There's so much to think about
That I cry, that I cry?'

Second Musician

But her goodman answered her:
'Love would be a thing of naught
Had not all his limbs a stir
Born out of immoderate thought;
Were he anything by half,
Were his measure running dry.

> Lovers, if they may not laugh,
> Have to cry, have to cry.' [11]

MacDonagh sees this poem as further vindication of his claim that Irish speech necessarily differentiates Irish poetry from English:

This poem is really syllabic, seven syllables to the line, like one species of Debhidhe poems in Irish—without, of course, the arrangements of assonance. I do not know if Mr. Yeats is aware of this syllabic measure; but again and again in his poems and in the poems of many contemporary Irishmen I find this tendency. Indeed I should say that the effects of our more deliberate Irish speech on our verse are these two: first, a prose intonation, not monotonous, being saved by the natural rise and fall of the voice, a remnant of the ancient pitch—a quality, as it were, of chanted speech—and second, a tendency to give in certain poems, generally of short riming lines, almost equal stress to all the syllables, a tendency to make the line the metrical unit. From the first of these effects comes a more reasoning, not to say conversational tone, which disallows inversions, quaint words and turns of speech. Not conforming in our way of verse to the regular English stress rhythm we have not the same necessity as the English poets to depart from the natural word order. We have not to manufacture a rhythm in that unnatural way.[12]

The division here made by MacDonagh between verse written in accord with the "natural rise and fall of the voice" and verse written by syllabic count with all syllables receiving almost equal stress is a division peculiarly fitting to Yeats's verse. It is ironic, however, that MacDonagh should have chosen this particular poem, for the closing line of each stanza has only six syllables. My own understanding of this song's prosody is that all but the last lines have seven syllables *and* four major stresses; the apparently anomalous lines have only six syllables but four major stresses, and their deviation from strict syllable count is compensated for by their conformity to the four-stress norm. The poem has a mixed prosody, as many of Yeats's poems do.

The proper ratio of naturalness to formality cannot be fixed in any rigorously systematic manner, but Yeats was constantly seeking the unique and intuitively felt ratio that would endow each poetic structure with its appropriate form. His rhymes reflect his preoccupation, for they are rhymes, clearly enough, but often very imperfect. One poem has the following rhyme pattern:

A	flare
A	ear
B	room
A	bore
B	womb
A	shows
A	knows
B	walk
A	clothes
B	talk
A	pains
A	sustains
B	stop
A	bones
B	up [13]

This is far from atypical of a rhyming habit that can produce such combinations as "gone–stone–sun," "intent–point," "house–luminous," "thought–begot," "on–man–Lane," all in one very formal poem. Because of his intent concern with meaning, and because his rhyme words often controlled meaning and established tone, his persistent assonance does not seem forced. Professor Wimsatt has discussed the novelty generated by Pope's refusal to rhyme noun with noun or verb with verb, so that the expected rhyming sound continued surprising through centuries of couplets. Yeats achieved the opposite effect by upsetting the ear's expectancies and fulfilling the emotional currents of meaning:

> The light of evening, Lissadell,
> Great windows open to the south,
> Two girls in silk kimonos, both
> Beautiful, one a gazelle.[14]

Here the off-rhyme of "both" with "south" is rhetorically predictable by the antecedent "Two girls," and when the full rhyme comes, it does not clang heavily because the carryover of the preceding line holds the gazelle in its web. I do not mean by this that the rhymes are to be unnoticed, merely that they are to be seen as part of the line. The importance of this linear unity is engrossed by Yeats's tendency to present his matter in a long and overriding period. The result is a great deal of rhetorical repetition within a given stanza, fortified and at times undercut by the poetics, the insistence on linear form rather than periodic. In the reminiscent poems this is especially evident, and when in his commemorative poem for Eva Gore-Booth and Con Markiewicz he returns to the initial image of the two girls in silk kimonos, the repetition is qualified by the use of off-rhyme:

> Many a time I think to seek
> One or the other out and speak
> Of that old Georgian mansion, mix
> Pictures of the mind, recall

> That table and the talk of youth,
> Two girls in silk kimonos, both
> Beautiful, one a gazelle.[15]

As with all his refrains, this repetition is so changed by its context that its meaning has shifted, in this instance, from the original exaltation to muted sadness. The development of the poem has been a major force, and the rhyme of "recall–gazelle" merely fortifies the resigned imperfection of life so far presented. And since the initial image of the girls at the south window has been revised and qualified by the overlay of their later experience, the term "recall" implies effortfulness in evocation, and what was so sweetly and spontaneously present initially has by now become soiled and darkened by the irrelevancies of life. The imperfect rhyme is consonant with the imperfections of experience that have led from the prized recollection to this hesitant attempt to bring back to mind what had once occurred without conscious thought.

But Yeats's off-rhymes were not justified by one specific motive. Frequently they did exhibit an imperfection in the experience treated:

> . . . the children's eyes
> In momentary wonder stare upon
> A sixty-year old smiling public man.[16]

This presentation of his own image as comical is matched by the awkwardness of "upon–man," but the same sort of self-deprecation is, later in the poem, presented in perfect rhyme:

> Better to smile on all that smile, and show
> There is a comfortable kind of old scarecrow.[17]

Not every sardonic statement occurs in off-rhyme, though many do:

> But the torn petals strew the garden plot
> And there's but common greenness after that.[18]

The justification of off-rhyme comes not in any single relation between tone and rhyme, but in the appropriateness to line and stanza. No irony is intended in the first stanza of "Crazy Jane and Jack the Journeyman" when "bone" is rhymed with "gone," and when two-thirds of the rhymes in the very carefully written "Coole Park, 1929" are imperfect, that is no reason for suspecting a self-deprecating intent.

We do not, in reading Yeats's later poems, think of the off-rhymes as violations of perfection. They are too normal, too pervasive in the poetry's texture, to come as violations of expectation. When he rhymes, in "Sailing to Byzantium," "young" with "song" and "dress" with "'magnificence" and "soul" with "animal," no principle is violated, no convention flaunted. The rhymes require no more justification than do perfect rhymes, for they are striking only in their appropriateness.

With these provisos, it is still possible to see Yeats's off-rhymes as indices to his state of mind. In his early poems, the extremely rare off-rhymes asked to be forgiven, and this was easy enough to do on the infrequent occasions when charity required it. They were simply the sort of thing that is, at times, necessary. After the 1903 volume, the frequency of off-rhyme increased until off-rhyme became a predictable part of the expectations of any reader of Yeats's verse. But like all the technical changes in Yeats's verse, this major shift was tightly bound up with the changes in the quality of experience that he took to be poetically admissible. The off-rhymes are comic not in the conventional sense but in the Yeatsean sense that they admit the presence of a world of divided imperfection, and the language of that world. They were part of his refusal to be ingratiating, and they were means of indicating the precedent claims of fullness. And these off-rhymes were not mere failures, second-best choices that he used only after he had tried unsuccessfully to make perfect rhymes. One of his habits in composing was to establish his possible rhymes and write to them, fill out the design thus offered. The rhyming of "bough" with "dew" in the second part of "Vacillation" was established early in the manuscript drafts, and when he wrote out a set of rhymes for this stanza, he accepted the rhyme without trouble:

> bough
> leaf
> dew
> chief
> anew
> belief
> grief [19]

And though he changed "anew" to "renew" and altered "leaf," "chief," and "belief," he accepted "bough" and "dew." He was not deterred by their obvious imperfection.

He did not say, "Well, let's rough it up a bit here and make it awkward there; that will make it seem mussed and *real*." The truth was that the off-rhymes were to his mind normal, not violations of convention but in effect the establishment of patterns that were in themselves valid. They made his already tightly linked —by internal sound pattern, by syntax—poems more linear. The assonant rhymes of Wilfred Owen, by contrast, do not make the poems linear but instead call attention, by their insistent harshness, to themselves. With Owen, we are always aware that the poems are rhyming very oddly; with Yeats, we know that they rhyme, but we see the rhyme, important as it is, as part of a general interweaving of sound and assertion. One virtue of his prosody is its insistence on the line as unit, and off-rhyme was a device strengthening this insistence.

His stanzaic habits are also rather fixed. He wrote only two sonnets in his later years, and in his lyrics he wrote practically no free verse. One of his favorite stanza forms ("Sailing to Byzantium," "Among School Children," parts II and III of "Vacillation") was the *ottava rima*, which he handled with extraordinary skill. Some of his stanza forms were taken from minor earlier writers, as the form of "In Memory of Major Robert Gregory" was taken from Cowley's "Ode on the Death of Mr. William Hervey" and used again in "A Dialogue of Self and Soul" and part II of "The Tower." The stanza form of "The Mother of God" also came from Cowley, for under his first notes on the poem's subject appears a brief description of the stanza used by Cowley in the lyric from his "Essay on Solitude":

5 feet good
4   "   wood
4   "   rejoice
5   "   voice
3   "   food [20]

Yeats evidently meant by "feet" stresses, as his finished poem shows:

> The threefold terror of love; a fallen flare
> Through the hollow of an ear;
> Wings beating about the room;
> The terror of all terrors that I bore
> The Heavens in my womb.[21]

In this one poem, and in no other, he followed the pattern of rhymes and of line length established by Cowley's lyric. Other stanza forms, like the elaborate form of part III of "Nineteen Hundred and Nineteen," were evidently invented for the occasion. He frequently, especially in the short lyrics, wrote in quatrains. He preferred stanzaic form that was fairly elaborate and compelled him to feats of self-discipline. Characteristically in his manuscripts he wrote out the rhyme scheme in ABC form, and he often wrote the rhymes for a stanza (altering as he went along) before writing all the lines.

The general design of his later prosody suggests that his primary aim was to effect a passionate syntax that would allow the voice to move in proximity to authentic patterns of speech. His steady use of off-rhyme is one indication of this motive, as is his occasional departure from the linear norm established in the poem, the use of an extra stress in a stress line, the occasional redundant syllable in a syllabic line. The off-rhymes indicated his primary interest in getting the semantics of a poem right, and his use of stanza forms that require repeated rhyme (notably the ottava rima) permitted him to use off-rhyme without obvious insistence. Within the elaborate stanza form, the off-rhymes were separated by intervening lines, and Yeats's special urge toward making stanza and sentence coincide made the stanza a more naturally fluent structure.

Stanzaic formality was necessary to him for many reasons, but chiefly he required it as discipline for the passionate syntax that he accepted as a norm. In his prosody as in his iconography he qualified his motives in dramatic terms. In the only recently published preface to the projected 1936 edition of his poems he talks at some length about his sense of prosody and characteristically prefaces his comments with notes on lyric dramaturgy:

> Style is almost unconscious. I know what I have tried to do, little what I have done. Contemporary lyric poems, even those that move me—"The Stream's Secret," "Dolores"—seemed too long, but an Irish preference for a swift current might be mere indolence, yet Burns may have felt the same when he read Thompson (*sic*) and Cowper. The English mind is meditative, rich, deliberate, it may remember the Thames valley. I planned to write short lyrics or poetic drama where every speech would be short and concentrated, knit by dramatic tension, and I did so with more confidence because young English poets were at that time writing out of emotion at the moment of crisis, though their old slow-moving meditation returned almost at once. Then, and in this English poetry has followed my lead, I tried to make the language of poetry coincide with that of passionate, normal speech. I wanted to write in whatever language comes most naturally when we soliloquise, as I do all day long, upon the events of our own lives or of any life where we can see ourselves for the moment. I sometimes compare myself with the mad old slum women I hear denouncing and remembering; "How dare you," I heard one say of some imaginary suitor, "and you without health or a home!" If I spoke my thoughts aloud they might be as angry and as wild.[22]

But anger and wildness were not the end product of poetry, and the function of traditional meters was to qualify, condition, and purify these originating motives. The powerful syntax that he thought desirable would be formalized by stanzaic pattern, and out of the tension of pattern and passion would come a permanent joyful poetry:

It was a long time before I had made a language to my liking; I began to make it when I discovered some twenty years ago that I must seek, not as Wordsworth thought, words in common use, but a powerful and passionate syntax, and a complete coincidence between period and stanza. Because I need a passionate syntax for passionate subject-matter I compel myself to accept those traditional metres that have developed with the language. Ezra Pound, Turner, Lawrence wrote admirable free verse, I could not. I would lose myself, become joyless like those mad old women. The translators of the Bible, Sir Thomas Browne, certain translators from the Greek when translators still bothered about rhythm, created a form midway between verse and prose that seems natural to impersonal meditation; but all that is personal soon rots; it must be packed in ice or salt. . . . If I wrote of personal love or sorrow in free verse, or in any rhythm that left it unchanged, amid all its accidence, I would be full of self-contempt because of my egotism and indiscretion, and foresee the boredom of my reader. I must choose a traditional stanza, even what I alter must seem traditional. . . .[23]

This passage suggests the theoretical justification of his practice that Yeats came to at the close of his career. It suggests also the main motive of this chapter, to explore through printed and manuscript versions of Yeats's later poems the way in which he established a prosody at once traditional and innovative, flexible to his extremely varied needs as poet, and capable of endowing his passionate articulations with a form that would make them seem ". . . all men's speech."

The Stress of Song

The prosodic possibilities available to Yeats as a poet writing in English were four in number. He could conceive of the line as written in feet, chiefly iambic, and he could attempt to maintain a set number of feet per line, as in the standard iambic pentameter. He could count syllables and keep a fixed syllable count of six, eight, ten, any given number, to a line. Or he could ignore syllable count or the concept of the foot and simply maintain a relatively fixed number of heavy stresses per line, with wide range of syllable count. Or he could ignore any fixed count of foot, stress, or syllable and write in free verse, using breath and phrase as prosodic units. It has always seemed to me peculiarly fruitless to exert on Yeats's verse the norms of foot meter, and to be quite frank I am extremely skeptical of the value of scanning most English verse by breaking it down into patterns of syllables that form something called feet. I find no positive evidence that Yeats thought in terms of feet, and my own persuasion is that he combined a syllabic and a stress prosody. In such a prosody a five-stress line is the equivalent of a ten-syllable line, and the two are interchangeable. The ten-syllable line may have in it well over five stresses; the five-stress line may have more or less than ten syllables; but they are equivalent. Any given poem may be in one or the other measure predominantly, and in Yeats's prosody there tends to be a correlation between the kind of poem and the kind of line used. His more formal, commemorative, and meditative poems tend to

be in decasyllabic lines that give them their air of philosophic weight and contemplative grasp. His brief intense lyrics, on the other hand, are written in lines that
are best understood as being divisible into a fixed number of stresses, with a wide range of syllable count.

One fine example of a poem written in a three-stress
line is "Mohini Chatterjee," which has often been compared with a very early Yeats poem, "Kanva on Himself." Although I am not here primarily concerned with
Yeats's development from his early work, "Kanva" is
so illuminating a contrast and suggests so clearly the
vigor of his later prosody that it seems useful to reprint it:

> Now wherefore hast thou tears innumerous?
> Hast thou not known all sorrow and delight
> Wandering of yore in forests rumorous,
> Beneath the flaming eyeballs of the night,
>
> And as a slave been wakeful in the halls
> Of Rajas and Mahrajas beyond number?
> Hast thou not ruled among the gilded walls?
> Hast thou not known a Raja's dreamless slumber?
>
> Hast thou not sat of yore upon the knees
> Of myriads of beloveds, and on thine
> Have not a myriad swayed below strange trees
> In other lives? Hast thou not quaffed old wine
>
> By tables that were fallen into dust
> Ere yonder palm commenced his thousand years?
> Is not thy body but the garnered rust
> Of ancient passions and of ancient fears?
>
> Then wherefore fear the usury of Time,
> Or Death that cometh with the next life-key?

Nay, rise and flatter her with golden rhyme,
For as things were so shall things ever be.[24]

Many young poetic aspirants are pleased by this poem,
for, if Yeats once wrote so badly, the Nobel Prize may
not be past their reach. The padded lines, the funny
images, the unspeakable statements ("Or Death that
cometh with the next life-key"), the closing platitude,
the weary archaisms, the twisted syntax—it is a perfect
compendium of faults. In the early drafts of the second
part of "Mohini Chatterjee," some of these characteristics were carried over, and the excision of them was
one of his major motives. The first section began easily,
following a prose draft:

What prayers should I pray? Do not pray, said the Brahmin
but say I have been man and woman, king and slave, myriad of
beloveds have sat on my knees, I have sat on a myriad knees
and shudder thinking that soon I must change again always as
insect in the roots of the grass.[25]

He then wrote a draft, underpunctuated but close to
the final version:

> I asked if I should pray
> But the Brahmin said
> "Pray for nothing, say
> Every night in bed
> 'I have been a king
> I have been a slave
> Nor is there anything

> a. Any fool, rascal, knave
> b. Fool, rascal, knave

> a. I have not been
> b. That I have not been

> And yet upon my breast
> A myriad heads have lain.' "

It is characteristic of Yeats's manuscripts that the original versions of poems should be underpunctuated, for he evidently felt no need to indicate syntactic pauses at the close of lines: the ending of a line automatically indicated a pause. The revision of line 8 shows Yeats excising a redundant word, diminishing the number of syllables in the line and exerting heavier stress on individual words, and it is a vivid example of the way that he manipulated lines, relying on the uniformity of stress pattern to justify the variation of syllables. The problems posed by the second part of the poem, however, did not involve filing and heightening but choosing situation, icon, and moral judgment.

What he had settled in the first section of "Mohini Chatterjee" was its rhythmic norm, and this controlled whatever suggestions came to his mind for incorporating judgments fundamentally similar to those in "Kanva on Himself." Having made the utterance, he sought to identify the speaker:

> A stranger with strange eyes
> Murmured in my youth
> These or words like these
> And add then to that
> All that has been shall be

He was trying to find a three-stress equivalent to "And as things are so shall they ever be." He gave up trying to characterize his speaker after another false try ("Mohini Chatterjee / A young handsome man / Spoke these or words like these"), and concentrated on the meaning of the statement:

> I heard those words in youth
> a. And never have I found
> b. And much have thought thereon

    a. A more majestic truth
    b. But found no better truth

       So wherefore groan and moan
       About old wrong (?)
       Seeing there's time for all

Not satisfied with the abstract statement, and certainly not satisfied with the "wherefore" of "Kanva on Himself," so inappropriate to this new utterance, he sought out more concrete data and fixed on the image of the lovers:

> Feet that once were light
>
> Eyes that once were bright
>
> Feet
>
> Eyes
>
> Eyes remembered bright
>
> Feet in old days light shall
>
> Shall once
>
> Once more be light and bright
>
> Once more be bright or light

A Foot

All

All that

    a. Lovers or companions
    b. All old companions

    a. Living and dying side
    b. Live side by side
    c. Be once more side by side

       The starry circuit run

    a. Till they be satisfied
    b. That they be satisfied

Of all these efforts, only the very last ("That they be satisfied") won a place in the final version. The rest were put aside, the feet and eyes because too literally "abstract" from the meanings and figures intended, although the "feet" would reappear in the final version and be integrated with the figure of repeated design suggested by the "starry circuit." But the eyes and feet that, these notes suggest, were to be rekindled and re-animated were assimilated into the lovers who, in the final version, would gain in the whole pattern of time what they were not granted in their single segment. These notes were conceptual statements: lovers will not be eternally separated because the larger designs of the universe favor their fulfillment.

The facing page of the notebook establishes yet another concern of the poem while reinforcing the concept of the circuit, which is here seen as "human" or "mortal" rather than "starry," though it is still a dominant force: "The circuit sets the pace." The fresh concern, which balances love, is war:

> Old soldiers face to face
> a. And every fight fought (?) out
> b. Every fight fought out
> c. All old fights fought out
> The circuit sets the pace
> For strategic thought

Both lover and warrior live within the "circuit" that sets the tempo of experience. Trying to bring the two together, he was driven to an exclamation: "Aye life oh life." And trying to see war and love as one unit, he saw them first as expressions of emotion—love—versus reason—war ("Whether in thought or desire")—but then altered the phrasing to fix both love and war as the expressions of passion, "Whether from hate or desire." He could then see the two as part of a large design of death and birth:

> By a myriad of births
> By a myriad of deaths
>
> Then by a myriad births
> A myriad graves appear
>
> A myriad of births
> A myriad of graves

So end the preliminaries to the ultimate composing of the poem. What we have witnessed, so far as the manuscripts and my imagination can take us, is the refinement of a subject suggested by the original "Kanva on Himself," beginning with a prose redaction of the occasion that gave rise to the early poem, followed by a versification of Chatterjee's speech. This versification established a norm of three stresses for the poem, and within that norm Yeats was committed to work. His rejection of the "feet" and "eyes" of these notes may in part have come from the impossibility of accommodating them to the three-stress line:

> Eyes remembered bright
>
> Feet in old days light shall
>
> Shall once
>
> Once more be light and bright

The modal "shall" presented a prosodic problem not worth working on, and that fact combined with the abstractness of statement to let him jettison "eyes" and "feet."

Out of this process emerged the completed poem, and that process was lifelong, both in technical development and in the scrutiny of obsessive pattern. The design of the dance, the faith in a cosmos of continuing life, the prideful assertion of self, the sense of circularity, the admiring emphasis on the irrational—these are familiar elements in the body of Yeats's work. The prosody, at once so simple and so adaptable, so free and so structured, makes vocalic and immediate these motives. In spite of the Brahmin's advice against praying, the poem is prayerful in the sense that it invokes powers resident in the person but latent unless brought into existence by language. The commentary is a declaration that willfully creates the conditions it describes and identifies the poet with the Brahmin and the sages, makes him a sayer as well as seer:

> I asked if I should pray,
> But the Brahmin said,
> 'Pray for nothing, say
> Every night in bed,
> "I have been a king,
> I have been a slave,
> Nor is there anything,
> Fool, rascal, knave,
> That I have not been,
> And yet upon my breast
> A myriad heads have lain." '
>
> That he might set at rest
> A boy's turbulent days
> Mohini Chatterjee
> Spoke these, or words like these.

> I add in commentary,
> 'Old lovers yet may have
> All that time denied—
> Grave is heaped on grave
> That they be satisfied—
> Over the blackened earth
> The old troops parade,
> Birth is heaped on birth
> That such cannonade
> May thunder time away,
> Birth-hour and death-hour meet,
> Or, as great sages say,
> Men dance on deathless feet.'

The syllable count ranges from four ("Fool, rascal, knave") to seven ("A myriad heads have lain"), but most of the lines have three major stresses. The certain exceptions are the last two lines, each of which has four stresses:

> Or, as great sages say,
> Men dance on deathless feet.

But these two lines and the preceding one ("Birth-hour and death-hour meet"), which might also be construed as having four major stresses, have six syllables only. This substitution of a six-syllable line for a three-stress line is so common a practice in Yeats's later verse that we might think of it as a convention of the poetry. The principle of linear substitution grants his work extraordinary flexibility.

In some of his lyrics the complications of this prosody are extraordinary, and one high point is "Crazy Jane and Jack the Journeyman." I have already discussed one account of the poem's origins in Yeats's visionary experience. In the context of "Words for Music Perhaps," part of the poem's impact comes from its dramatization of the anti-Christian Black Mass of Eden that underlies that series and in which Jane and Jack are primary embodiments of Yeats's argument for a religion of ignorance. The poem is so deliberately committed to bodily earthly life that it even denies the paganism of the Neo-Platonist. But the poem began with rather different motives. It was at first part of the long argument between man and woman that Yeats found an obsessive subject, Jack declaring the immortality of his love, Jane skeptically (and ruefully) giving him the lie.

> Wild Jack when he was drunk
> Said love could never die
>
> Half drunk he cried that such a love
> Outlived moon and sun;
> I stamped my foot and cried in rage
> Easy got and gone

The argument was then phrased in dialogue form:

> **She**
> "The more I leave the door unlatched
> The sooner love is gone"
> **He**
> What matter though a look can make
> Me tremble in my bone

This implied argument with its suggestive sexual overtones forms the base of the final poem, which acts as an aftermath to a prior quarrel. The crystallizing element in the poem's construction was the phrase "the door unlatched," and its peculiarly haunting rhythm, echoed at first by "look can make" and later more effectively by

"when looks meet." The key phrase was at first not leading and dominant:

> Half drunk he cried that such a love
> Outlived moon and sun

But when he turned to concentrated composing he
noted his key rhythmic phrase first:

> The more I leave the door unlatched
> The sooner love is gone
> Although a look can make

Attacking the opening once again he worked toward
shaping a line that would parallel his guiding rhythm:

> I know although this eye can make
> Me tremble to the bone

> I know although this eye can make
> Of life mockery

> I know although when look meet look
> I tremble to the bone

And finally, with the underpunctuation so typical of
early drafts:

> I know although when looks meet
> I tremble to the bone
> The more I leave the door unlatched
> The sooner love is gone

The design of the poem was then established: an opening line of four major stresses, with two of those stresses
closely juxtaposed at the close of the line, this line followed by a three-stress line close to the conventional
rising pattern. The even lines rhyme, the odd lines do
not, and the syntax makes each pair of lines a unit of

meaning, so that the effect is of a single line broken.
There are, then, units within units, pairs of lines within
the stanza, lines within pairs, and the stanza identical
with the period. Within the longer lines, the divisions
are further intensified by the use of internal rhyme:

> I know although . . .
> The more I leave the door . . .

And within these units there are further interweavings
of sound, partly through end-rhyme, partly through
simple echo:

> I know, although when looks meet
> I tremble to the bone,
> The more I leave the door unlatched
> The sooner love is gone[,]
> For love is but a skein unwound
> Between the dark and dawn[.]

This stanza established the rhythmic pattern for the
poem, and from that point the problem of composition
diminished. Each stanza followed the same basic pattern, and the fifth line of the first and second stanzas
interlocked in rhyme with the (otherwise unrhyming)
third lines of the second and third stanzas. His only
difficulties came with the opening line of the second
stanza, where he tried "soul" at first before choosing
the primitive and in part depreciative "ghost," and with
the concluding stanza's form of address.

> A lonely ghost the ghost is
> That to God shall come;
> I—love's skein upon the ground,
> My body in the tomb—
> Shall leap into the light lost
> In my mother's womb.

> But were I left to lie alone
> In an empty bed,
> The skein so bound us ghost to ghost
> When he turned his head
> Passing on the road that night,
> Mine must walk when dead.

The difficulty with the concluding stanza grew in part from the remains of the original dialogue form of the poem, for even in the early printed versions the last stanza addressed Jack as "you," in spite of the poem's attempt to separate the living from the dead. In the completed context of the Crazy Jane series, intimate address was replaced by the dominant tone of public confession and outrage. The deliberate turning from the light to the dark community of sexual and earthly love is a declaration of commitment to death.

This poem, which I have always thought one of Yeats's greatest triumphs, is hardly exhausted by consideration of its prosody. But there seems to me no doubt that its impact as well as its evolution are conditioned by the most careful rhythmic discriminations that in a large sense controlled the poem's shaping. The rhythmic design is a major one in Yeats's later work, granting him the deep primitive simplicity of ballad meter ("Words for Music Perhaps") and the force of deliberate conscious shaping, so that the most simple and most sophisticated find common ground. Like Blake and Lawrence, Yeats had the capacity to think in designs that cut through the incrustations of modern life to those permanent realities that center and support our experience. His prosody was one major force that drove him to realities that other modern poets never genuinely reached. The pattern of "Crazy Jane and Jack the Journeyman" is in detail the pattern used in many of the poems in "A Man Young and Old" and *Last Poems,* but the basic stress prosody that underlies this poem and "Mohini Chatterjee" is a dominant mode in the verse that grants him access to a life at once strong and accurate, simple and sophisticated, passionate and intellectually magnificent.

The Articulation of Syllables

Yeats's verse, taken as a dramatic whole, moves "between extremities" always. The integrative aim figured by the centaur urged him toward projecting a total sense of possibility in prosody as in dramaturgy and iconography. His prosody allowed him to present through his stress lines the simple emotive expression of personified passions, the longer lines fixed mainly by syllabic count expressing the meditation of the civilized intellect.

In his syllabic as in his stress prosody, the guiding motives were the passionate syntax of the sentence, which was in turn qualified by stanzaic pattern and his tendency toward making stanza and period coincide. The same compensations already noted in his stress prosody operated in lines governed mainly by syllable count. Just as in the last three lines of "Mohini Chatterjee" he substituted lines of six syllables and four stresses for the normal three-stress line, he would in writing a poem in decasyllables feel free to substitute a five-stress line when the emergencies of syntax required it. For his poems, the concept of the iambic line with variable feet is ugly and redundant, and, since simple hypotheses are most elegant and most useful, the best prosodic hypothesis for poems like "Sailing to Byzantium" and "Among School Children" is that he wrote them in lines of ten syllables. What minor deviations occur can be accommodated by assuming that he often slurred (elided) a weakly stressed syllable and sometimes substituted a five-stress for a ten-syllable line.

In composing, Yeats at first wrote his decasyllables in a loose form, often merely filling out a line to satisfy the prescribed rhyme scheme so that he could maintain his momentum. He then reduced syllabic redundancy as much as possible until he had so concentrated a line that each syllable was carrying weight and the line was normally reduced to ten syllables. I have already cited above the alteration in "Among School Children" that causes some syntactic confusion:

> And that must sleep or struggle to escape
>
> And that must sleep, shriek, struggle to escape

Here the addition of *shriek* is not necessary for propriety if one is merely concerned with the norm of the foot, but it is needed by the criterion of reducing redundancy and giving each syllable as much semantic weight as it can carry. The difference between the first draft and the final version of a single ottava rima stanza—and a reasonably characteristic one—shows how his mind worked over and altered flaccid lines:

> We too had many pretty toys when young:
> A law indifferent to blame or praise,
> A speedy remedy to obvious wrong
> No swaggering soldier on the public ways

> Who weighed a man's life lighter than a song;
> A general confidence in future days
> In some great thing to come, because we thought
> That the worst rogues and rascals had died out.

Of these lines (in "Nineteen Hundred and Nineteen"),
only the first two and the last would survive. Some lines
he reshaped in order to develop concepts relevant to
the preceding stanza; from others he excised certain
figures because, as matters developed, they would fit
more properly in following stanzas. But generally, he
changed in order to get the densest possible semantic
arrangement within a decasyllabic line:

> We too had many pretty toys when young:
> A law indifferent to blame or praise,
> To bribe or threat; habits that made old wrong
> Melt down, as it were wax in the sun's rays,
> Public opinion ripening for so long
> We thought it would outlive all future days.
> O what fine thought we had because we thought
> That the worst rogues and rascals had died out.

In part the changes were warranted by changes in the
first stanza, for the third line of the first stanza had at
one point noted the "insolence of the sun"; but when the
poem had progressed to the point of the second stanza,
the sun could be removed from the first stanza and appear here in the function that Yeats more systematically
endowed it with: that of representative of the rational
faculty. The line that gave him this opening was the
extremely flaccid "A speedy remedy to obvious wrong,"
for, even if we take the line to be ironic, why should
we expend irony on such flabbiness? The objects of
Yeats's contempt have at least to be worthy of it. The
swaggering soldier could also be put off, as his proper

function in succeeding stanzas was revealed. Hence the second stanza could serve the role of balancing against the "ingenious lovely things" that seemed "sheer miracle" to the Grecian populace the habits and laws that with public opinion were supposed equally to work miracles for the European world before 1914. The statement, at once sympathetic and mocking, makes the abstractions of law, habit, and public opinion equivalent to the concretions of Athena's image, the ivories of Phidias, and the golden grasshoppers and bees, both object and abstraction being defenseless against the circle of the moon and the whirling dust of history. To make the stanza an appropriate contrast, he had to identify himself with the aspirations of pre-war Europe while making clear their futility.

The motivation for change was, then, not simply prosodic but conditioned by the metaphorical structure of the entire poem and by Yeats's sense of his special position as spokesman—participant and articulator. What resulted was a stanza of decasyllabic lines in which a deliberate voice evaluated precisely and economically a wide context of experience. The difference between original and final lines demonstrates the forceful economy of his control of the line:

a. A spéedy rémedy to óbvious wróng

b. To bríbe or thréat; hábits that máde óld wróng

a. No swággering sóldier on the públic wáys

b. Mélt dówn, as it were wáx in the sún's ráys

a. A géneral cónfidence in fúture dáys

b. We thóught it wóuld outlíve áll fúture dáys

a. In sóme gréat thíng to cóme, becaúse we thóught

b. Ó what fíne thought we hád becaúse we thóught

The lines were thus established, basically decasyllabic, with as many major stresses as the syntax would bear.

One more stanza, the famous stanza on the divided tree in "Vacillation," is so indicative of his habits of composition that it will serve as conclusion to this section. In this stanza, which I take as a microcosm of his habits, we can see Yeats's mind contemplating numerous possibilities, rejecting, seeking further, shaping the icon to suit the special definitive motives of the poem. We can see also the evolution of the stanza from inchoate potentiality to ultimate ordered prosodic shape. The stanza shows with remarkable clarity the kind of considerations he made.

"Vacillation" as a whole is composed of disparate yet central elements in Yeats's experience. Two sections of the poem—I and IV—come from earlier experience, stanza IV developing an experience of special intensity over fifteen years in the past, stanza I evidently coming out of an earlier period in his style and probably written some years before. In spite of the earlier origins of these sections of the poem, my own belief is that the occasion for the composition of the poem rose from his contemplation of the icon of the divided tree.

The sources of the icon are several, but the motive for its use is single. The tree is one of the most celebrated and most often remarked of Yeats's icons, and he used it frequently and throughout his career. Its importance is evident in the drafts of "Among School Children," where the briefly appearing hawthorn tree is asked whether it is all or the creator of all. The tree is a godlike force, and whether hawthorn, chestnut, or hazel, it has supernatural weight. Like birds, trees participated in a dual nature, rooted in earth, feeding on air, organic and fluent, between heaven and earth, self-complete. From his studies in Blake and in the cabala he learned of the dual trees of life and knowledge, and in the Mabinogion he learned of Peredur's divided tree and cited it in his essay (1897) on "The Celtic Element in Literature." He contemplated the tree in various forms throughout his lyrics, and he read of the tree of Attis in *The Golden Bough, Hastings' Encyclopedia of Religion and Ethics,* and Julian's hymn to the Great Mother of the Gods. The tree of Peredur was composed of two great opposites, moisture and fire, and, although in the Mabinogion it merely took its place as one more odd item in the landscape, Yeats by integrating it in his total understanding of the generic icon endowed it with rich connotations. The tree that eventually appeared in his poem was original in the sense that it was a new complex of elements, the pine tree of the priests of Gallus, the trees of life and of knowledge, Peredur's tree, and the organic form of the Romantic imagination. Several cultures were thus folded together into the special form required by Yeats's imagination.

His imagination in this poem was operating in a syncretic fashion similar to that already analyzed in "Lines Written in Dejection." For "Vacillation" is one of those synoptic poems that Yeats occasionally wrote to bring himself to momentary definition. Like the "Dialogue of Self and Soul," it considered the extremities of human experience and chose, in a deliberately good-humored manner, the extreme of commitment to unregenerated life. The fabled tree of this stanza becomes a center for opposed forces that live in a constant process of mutual feeding that can be transcended only by the interposition of the image of Attis. Hence the poem treats once again the puzzle that grows from the artist's necessity at once to transcend and to accept the limits of the generated soul.

His first notes on the tree are vague and inconclusive, although the initial line is settled:

> And And From its broad roots T its cry let out
> There is a tree that from its topmost bough
> > the other
> Is half flame, and one all one half a rusty flame,
> > > leaf
> > > leaf
> > > the other
> Is half all flame and half all abound all
> > > and half abounding leaf
> And half green
> That is for ever nourished with the dew
> The tree of knowledge mounts

In succeeding versions, several of these elements are conserved: the sense of abundance in the foliage, the presence of dew, the basic idea of the tree as divided equally into moisture and flame. The tree of knowledge, however, he saw to be not an adequate connotation for his inclusive intention. In conception the meaning of this central icon had not been established, and he had as yet no stanza form. The one relatively firm line— "There is a tree that from its topmost bough"—established the dominant form as decasyllabic, and it is possible that the obscure line concerned with the roots was tentatively placed as a possible rhyme of "out" and "bough." But the tree's roots would have no place in the final version.

On the page that contains his succeeding effort, a list
of rhymes appears:

> bough
> leaf   green
> dew
> chief   scene
> anew
> belief
> grief

What he evidently did was to take first the original
draft and note the two lines that were close to acceptable form, ending respectively in "bough" and
"leaf." He then filled out a general stanza scheme as a
working design and started to write to it:

> There is a tree ~~from~~ that from its topmost bough
> ~~all~~
> Is half all flame, and half all leafy green
>   the other leafy green
>
>   with
> That is for ever chilly in the dew
>
> So The

The substitution of "green" for the rhyme word "leaf"
compelled him to the revision of rhyme scheme, and as
he continued the poem even the new set of rhymes was
not appropriate. He still, in an unassimilated line, tried
to fill out a line to the rhyme word "scene." With the beginning line established, he turned to a new attack:

> Is one half glittering flame, the other green
> Abounding foliage moistened with the dew
>   They that
> And some let Attys image hang between

> Consuming flame and lush abounding leaf
> Know not what they know but know not grief.

With the beginning line, he had six completed lines, but as he observed the shape of the stanza it moved toward ottava rima, and he considered his second "B" line, using the rhyme word "scene" that his sketch of rhyme scheme had suggested:

> The tree of knowledge and of life and scene.

The tree was now more inclusive, not merely the tree of knowledge but also the tree of life. Hence he corrected his earlier notation, and in filling out the line to maintain his momentum and consider the possibilities implied by "scene," he learned what his tree would be. Knowledge and life, flame and dew—these were set, and in his drafts and in his noted rhyme scheme he had the following possibilities for pattern:

> bough
> green
> dew
> scene
> anew
> leaf
> grief

Thus he had established the ottava rima form, and the further development of the stanza was checked by this rhyme scheme:

> A tree there is and from the topmost bough
> One half is glittering flame, the other dewy green
> Abounding foliage moistened with the dew
> a. Knowledge and life made one for in the scene
> b. Wisdom displays all death but in the scene

   c. Wisdom has summoned death but in the scene
      What it destroys the foliage must renew
         He that
      And some like let Attys ancient image hang between
      They know not what they know but know not
   a. Consuming flame and the lush dewy leaf
   b. That staring fury and the blind lush leaf
      May know not what he knows but knows not grief

The evolution from the first notes growing from his various sources to the ultimate ottava rima stanza was by this point practically complete, and his main concern now was to clarify the relation between the staring fury and the blind lush leaf:

   A tree there is that from its topmost bough
   Is half all glittering flame and half all green
   Abounding foliage moistened with the dew;

   a. And half is half and yet is all the scene
   b. For ignorance and knowledge fill the scene
   c. But no not half for each is all the scene

   a. What one consumes the other can renew
   b. And half and half consume what they renew
   c. And what they most consume they most renew

   And he that Attys image hangs between
   That staring fury and the blind lush leaf
   not know not
   May mind now what he knows but knows no grief

He could then shape the first printed version:

   A tree there is that from its topmost bough
   Is half all glittering flame and half all green
   Abounding foliage moistened with the dew;
   And half is half and yet is all the scene;
   And half and half consume what they renew,
   And he that Attis' image hangs between

That staring fury and the blind lush leaf
May know not what he knows, but knows not grief.

What the evolution of this stanza shows is reasonably representative of the procedures that Yeats followed in establishing his highly formalized stanzaic patterns. Here he began with an icon of rich suggestiveness that expressed many of his basic preoccupations. He presented it to his imagination and contemplated it with fixed attention until he had formulated a linear statement that limited the possible rhythmic pattern to the decasyllabic form ("There is a tree that from its topmost bough"). With the primary conceptual statement made, so that the divided tree of Peredur became the physical reality of the stanza, he then sought out the implied stanzaic pattern, writing a list of rhyme words, and writing one line of nonsense in order to maintain the composing energy that both icon and prosody released. Within that stanza he was limited by rhyme scheme and the numerical limit of lines, and his problem was, accepting those limits, to implicate in the lines the greatest possible range of meaning. Hence his heavy abstraction in early drafts, the stress on wisdom, death, ignorance, knowledge, life, the attempt to gain inclusiveness by generality. The suppression of those overt concepts left the final version deliberately evasive and strangely mocking, even playful. The interchange of moisture and flame takes on the character of fluid dance, with equality set by the intervention of Attis' image, and the two extremities depreciated. In Yeats's several sources there is no reference to any "staring fury," and this is his way of identifying flame, death, and knowledge, each a destructive peril. And the blind lush leaf of ignorant life is seen as equally menacing to those who seek revelation beyond grief.

The lines, balanced in their movement, check and qualify the extremity of statement, so that the ultimate effect is tantalizing and haunting. His sources are thus reduced and arranged to a new shape. This is a tree that has been taken from Peredur and Attis so that it is no longer theirs, nor is it simply to be identified with the exemplary organic form that the Romantics—and Yeats in certain moods—took trees to be. The tree that he so certainly asserts to exist is ancient, dual, widely distributed in the folk religious imagination, associated with ritual practices, so inclusive as to subsume the twin trees of the cabala, and made up of both mere stupid persistent life and the all-revealing flame of deathful knowledge. The stanza has a wide and deliberately suppressed context. The deliberateness is shown in the substrata of thought present in the several rejected lines. The poet may tell all; but the stanza will not permit him to, for it forces compressions and omissions upon his merely personal will. The collision between the personal intent and the impersonal form generates a fresh tension.

The stanza is typical of Yeats's method of composing his decasyllabic lines. The stanza and the period coincide; the rhymes are guides to composition, and one pair is strikingly imperfect; the only lines that appear to have extra syllables are easily justified if one considers the natural elisions that take place in reading the lines aloud ("glittering" and "foliage" would easily slur to form two syllables each). "Vacillation" taken as a whole indicates the range of Yeats's prosody from the tight sparse stress lines of part I through the ottava rima of parts II and III, with their decasyllabic lines, and the stress lines of IV, V, and VI to the decasyllables of VII and thence to the rough fourteener of VIII. The inclusiveness that we have seen in his construction of the icon of the tree is exhibited throughout the poem, in the dramaturgy, the iconography, and the prosody. In its extraordinary ease and density, its sensitively varied texture, the poem represents one of Yeats's most revealing and rewarding works. He saw its theme as central to his view of experience, and his treatment of the icon of the tree, both in his sense of its connotations and in his disciplined ordering of the stanza, is indicative of the supreme integration of diverse materials and techniques that distinguished this poem and his entire career.

Anomalies

If we assume that Yeats used a dual prosody in which lines were justifiable by either stress or syllable count, and if we assume further that his concern with vocalic pressure and passionate syntax led him to minor violations of the decasyllabic line that can be accommodated by elision ("glittering," "foliage," "memory," "bodily"), then the anomalies in his lyric verse are remarkably few. The principle of linear substitution accounts for the peculiar prosodic structure of a poem like "Lapis Lazuli," where the eight-syllable and four-stress line have equal value and where he wins some of his most free and jubilant prosodic triumphs. There are, however, lines that violate even the wide range of expectations that my phrasing of his prosody allows. These lines occur with greater frequency in *Last Poems* than in *The Tower,* and there are two possible explanations. First, one might assume that the poems of his last years were not subjected to the same involved process of re-writing that gave many of his later poems that special quality of finish, even patina, that distinguishes his work. But this seems to me, in view of the extremely elaborate rewriting that underlay the printed versions of *Last Poems,* not a reasonable assumption. The second possibility, which seems to me more probable, is that the prosody of the poems after *The Winding Stair* displays the same effort toward liberation that I have already discussed in relation to his iconography. His growing recklessness, his increasing indifference to social judgment, is apparent in the dramaturgy and iconography of these final declarations, and the prosody exhibits the same motives. A line in one of his most celebrated poems shows his prosodic freedom. In "The Statues," after asserting that Pythagoras planned the statues and that there was then no reason for surprise or even for being attracted by the systematized forms of Greek statuary, he continued to talk in favor of an art of passion (personality) rather than of individualized character. These carefully engineered statues evoked responses that went deeper than any merely individual identity. And yet the statues presented a reality greater than any that Pythagoras could have construed, for all his intellectual brilliance:

> No! Greater than Pythagoras, for the men
> That with a mallet or a chisel modelled these
> Calculations that look but casual flesh, put down

All Asiatic vague immensities,
And not the banks of oars that swam upon
The many-headed foam at Salamis. . . .

The first two lines can be reasonably justified as having
five major stresses, and the last three are decasyllabic.
The one really anomalous line is "Calculations that look
but casual flesh," and even if we assume that Yeats
looked on "calculations" as having only one major stress
(a line in the fourth stanza of the poem confirms this),
the line is too heavily loaded to be justified even by
Yeats's very flexible prosody. One has to say either that
the line has five major loci of stress and is justifiable
only by a foot prosody, or one has to say that here
Yeats's prosody breaks down under the demands of his
syntax. What happened is, I think, an amalgamation of
these two possibilities. The phrase "Calculations that
look but casual flesh" has the weight and balance of a
Yeatsean line as well as the exact phrasing of one of his
obsessive aims. The phrase "put down" is by this very
fact given an extraordinary emphasis that is further
stressed by the suspended syntax. A passion that cannot be balked overpowers the formal requirement and
establishes another norm (that of the casual flesh?) that
distorts the expected shape. It can be justified prosodically but largely, I think, because we want to justify it,
because of its cogency and the articulation of the
stanza, rather than because of the norms of any prosody.

The anomalies merely dramatize the special qualities
of Yeats's prosody, for the simplicity and range of his
linear sense come directly from his concern with immediacy and permanence. In the minute discriminations of the line he sought the same reconciliation of
opposites that he reached toward in his quest for a

dramaturgy that would accept the peculiarities of his experience and the generality of his passions and for an iconography that would move with equal ease in the pageantry of cosmic process and the unreliable events of a fallen world. His syntax and prosody are the essential agents of his work, for it is in the pace and rhythm of language that poetry makes its most incisive effects. Each man has a prosody and syntax that limit the permissible relations of his language and thus condition his accessibility to experience. It is possible to change the dramatic or symbolic content of a mind and leave that mind essentially unchanged if no corresponding alteration of syntactic and rhythmic habits has been effected. The mind can always find equivalents to the exorcised symbols and remain as impervious as before. The mind's defenses are shrewd. Poetry, however, imposes a rhythm that impels the opening of new nervous channels, and it is the combination of syntax and prosody that ultimately liberates. The range of human possibility is limited by kinesthetic habit, and part of the resistance to poetry comes from a deep and justified conviction that it will make an exorbitant claim, will ask that we change our lives or, with overwhelmingly dangerous intimacy, force us to move in designs that until then we had neither entertained nor imagined. Yeats, moving within the main prosodic tradition of English, brought to it his highly charged and demanding apprehension of the fragmented mind in which we all participate, and he offered a troubling and suffering integrity to heal our inner divisions. The integrity of the prosody is the emblem of the wholeness and inclusiveness of his art, and of its insistence that we know ourselves and our condition afresh.

yeats and
contemporary poetry

Within the generation since his death, Yeats has become firmly established as one of the classic English poets. His value is little disputed, so that he has become a monument in the history of English poetry. The few negative critics—Yvor Winters or D. S. Savage—have had little effect; the most recent compendious anthology of modern poetry has no less than eighty poems by Yeats, and standard survey courses in English literature tend to conclude with generous representation of his verse.

At the same time his influence has been less than that of poets not so universally admired. There is a finish, an air of completeness to the complex architecture of his poetry, that implies an exhaustive use of idiom, and

232

his special intellectual ambience of heterodox mysticism attracts few of the younger writers. The elaborate meditations of Wallace Stevens and the instigations of Ezra Pound seem to leave open more possibilities in modern American idiom, and the conservative poetic mode of Robert Graves stands as a more imitable source of style for young British poets. In spite of his extensive comments on the art of poetry, Yeats has always seemed special and odd in his criticism, his pleas for Walter Pater and Dorothy Wellesley falling on suspicious ears, and his stress on magic lacking the kind of cultural acceptability that distinguishes the criticism of T. S. Eliot and his followers. And when an occasional critic speaks of the modern age as the Age of Yeats, he never sounds convincing. In a very real way, the greatest poet of the first half of the century seems out of place.

It is true that he participates in many of the excitements of the period: the concern with myth growing out of the anthropology of Frazer, Cornford, and Harrison; the absorption in Eastern thought; the preoccupation with theory of history; the essential isolation of the artist; the obsession with a natural syntax and diction; the reaction against the idea of progress; the quarrel between art and science; the search for a theory of symbolism; the acceptance of the concept of organic form; the urge toward the experimental. He participated in all these interests, and in some respects, notably in syntax and diction, he was a pioneer. But whatever his acceptance of modern subject matters and poetic problems, he remained withdrawn from the primary motives of much modern art. In that isolation, only partly ascribable to his special Irishness, he made a searching inspection of the modern poet's position.

In this book I have stressed the relevance of Yeats's poetics to the body of his work, as a way of indicating the range of possibilities that he allowed himself in writing. Beyond its usefulness for understanding Yeats's motives, the poetics can illuminate the work of other modern poets, especially those of our own period. His dramaturgy, for instance, comes from the most full examination of the relation between experience and artifact, and it has so great a range that it demonstrates in eloquent examples the problems faced by a modern man seriously shaping poetic forms. Except for translation, he practiced widely all the possible poetic enterprises, from objective drama to personal utterance, and he came in the process to certain conclusions that are applicable to our own poetry since, say, 1945.

Yeats's rejection of the categories of "individuality" and of "character" in favor of "personality" is not merely verbal crankiness. With certain vivid exceptions, the poetry of the recent past falls deliberately and fatally into the categories of poetry written out of character (dandyism) and poetry written out of willed individuality (hipsterism), both involving a primary reaction to social realities that in Yeats's terms is either pre-poetic or not poetic at all, not concerned with that deposit of subject matter from which no artist can separate himself without radical damage. Writing of recent British literature Giorgio Melchiori saw it as the work of tightrope walkers, and, once that image is fixed in the mind, it is amazing how much of recent American writing, especially poetry, is concerned with funambulistes and jugglers, how often the pointlessness and necessity of elaborate tricks to keep balance appear.

Balance of this sort is a simple refuge from disaster, and there is no reason for retaining it other than habit and upbringing. The mode of balancing, that is, elaboration and cataloguing on the one hand, formalizing through already existent artifacts on the other, varies as does the audience toward which the poetry is directed, and the poetry merely plays on established habits. The poetry of character and the poetry of individuality are equally conventional because they imply a prior agreement between audience and poet, a piety. The pleasure taken by an audience in the poetry of Allen Ginsberg and Gregory Corso depends on the degree to which that audience is delighted to see certain pieties (which they have rejected) violated, but the difference between piety and impiousness has never seemed to me very great. And the pleasure that Richard Wilbur's poetry evokes is primarily pleasure in the agreed agreeably beautiful, delicate nature, baroque fountains, rococo gardens, the poet as juggler of beautifully tinted objects that intoxicate the imagination with memory of officially certified loveliness. Poets who are maintaining a habit of morale and poets who are attacking those habits are social poets. As most poets are. "Personality," in Yeats's sense of the term, is an extremely rare phenomenon. The bulk of poetry—the bulk of Yeats's poetry—moves within the categories of character and individuality; that is, it has a primarily social reference. For, once poetry has attained a certain level of professional competence, it is lifted from the ruck to the extent that it is "distinguished," that is, recognizably placed in a convention established by preceding authors. The model grants character, and to witness that character stamped successively on new subjects by the force of parody or application of set style is a source of knowledge. The pleasure of recognition and certification of interest, the reminder of what measures and controls and revelations a certain style compels, the sense of familiarity—these are poetic rewards. At their worst, they are sheer obvious conventionalities and evoke a kind of weary respect, but in the work of accomplished writers they more frequently evoke a kind of indolent amusement, a happy illusion of communal habit.

The poetry of character and the poetry of individuality are two sides of a single coin. For if the poetry of character is a reminder of agreement, the poetry of individuality simply denies the agreements established by the social contract. But rather than opting out of the society, it remains bound to the structure and exists chiefly as irritative and reactive force. It expresses that immense reservoir of bad feeling which social decorum very properly keeps out of the realms of organized conduct, and when decorum becomes frigid and pointlessly repressive, this reservoir seethes and ultimately explodes. And such explosions serve a social function—they are otherwise certainly not justifiable. The two chief recent loci for such explosions are John Osborne's *Look Back in Anger* and Allen Ginsberg's *Howl.*

To confine the matter arbitrarily to poetry and America, the title poem of *Howl* displays clearly the relation

between character and individuality in a poet's dramaturgy, for the protagonist of that poem is the poet ex-
pelled from the academy "for crazy," and Carl Solomon
alone and hallucinated in the insane asylum is the
blood brother of the secure suburbanite pridefully sur-
rounded by his carefully clipped lawn rather than a
cyclone fence: "ah, Carl, while you are not safe I am
not safe. . . ." The systematic assault on the smug
security of the suburbanite, the attempt to call attention to the abyss at his feet and his identity with the
insane who are committed to slightly different but inter-
connected institutions—this is the poem's base, and it is
founded on the very sand that it dislikes. To be "anti-
academic" is in effect to honor the academy, at least to
expend considerable emotional energy on it. And *Howl*
is intentionally anti-academic and anti-institutional. Its
resentments and rejections take their meaning from the
context out of which the poem rises, namely, the steady
march of ambitious, intelligent young men from preparatory school to their ultimate apotheosis in academies,
laboratories, courts, bureaus, clinics, and factories,
where their chosen brains can operate most effectively
to keep society at its highest possible technological
level. The deviation from that march it describes as
existent and valuable and imminent for all, and its chief
offensiveness comes from its ascription of value to what
is, in that particular order of things, anathema.

Howl meant to be offensive. That, under the fuss
about obscenity and the religiosity of the poem, was the
main point. The religious motive and the generous compassion, which were real and deep in the poem's design, were also modes of counterbalancing the explicit

charge of the poem that under the false order was none
at all, that the square of lawn was as meaningless a
protection as the cyclone fence, that the fence protected neither inmate nor society, that the lawn confined the inhabitant in madness.

The poem reflected the social and psychological disorders that other poems elegant and dandyish had by
their determined evasions also reflected. It was the
world that they suppressed, and its therapeutic insistence on diseased life was an appeal for direct diversion
of attention. In it the poet stood apart and bore witness
to the suffering and sordid life that the official culture
blandly ignored. And this was done with such passion,
wit, and eloquence as to be profoundly troubling and
impressive.

My respect for *Howl,* like my respect for Richard
Wilbur's *The Beautiful Changes,* is considerable. They
define, clarify, and bring poetically to attention concerns that are necessarily those of any cultivated man
in this age. They may be concerns that, finally, any
given person might consign to oblivion or minor emphasis, but to ignore or dismiss them abruptly is to deny
one's historical identity. But it is precisely there that
their limitations are fixed and they fail to exhaust the
total integral possibilities of poetry, character and individuality being social categories that are time-
devoured. And in less competent hands than Wilbur's
the poetry of character comes to appear like the great
mass of poetry written by American divines in the late
seventeenth and early eighteenth centuries, the over-
flow of pointless leisure and unengaged intellectual

force. And when Ginsberg's materials are treated by sensibilities less immersed in poetic discipline, the results are the vulgarly self-indulgent expressions of self-hatred, grudges, disgust, and rant that increasingly clutter the pages of the less distinguished little magazines.

What then is left? For it is possible to assert with good reason that poetry without some hope of social agreement is not possible, that the simple reference of the language can have no hope of establishing a community of response without a conventional set of associations. In this view, poetry is a non-originative social art that depends on *some* social milieu. To be the poet laureate of Bohemia or the class odist of the post-war academic world might be the extremes of possible success. American poetry at present may be the poetry of academic people carrying the fading torch of something called Western civilization and of Bohemians industriously tripping them up and hurling buckets of water on that guttering but stubborn flame.

The droll but not very pretty picture is fortunately not exhaustive. The tradition of "personality" which Yeats espoused has not died so easily that the field is given over entirely to poetry social in habit. The fact that the essentially prophetic and religious motives that Yeats saw as primary and that affected even his slightest lyrics are intermittent and hardly dominant in contemporary poetics should not come as a surprise. The motives are not easily brought over into form, and Yeats's own work testifies to the difficulty with which he labored to that end. In fact, one of the chief dramas of his work resides in the difficulties that he faced and the struggles toward the poetic that are exhibited in his greatest poems.

What Yeats implicitly required was a scale of values and range of knowledge that exceeded the limits of historic being, and after a brief concentration on the primitive residue of sign and persona that he found epitomized in Irish legend, he turned to detailed prolonged study of history, philosophy, and religion in an attempt to achieve a base of operation. And this base was not to be isolated from his sense of identity; it might clarify his standing and his role, but it would not deny his individual and social position. His five modes of poetic being (see pp. 42–57 above) were several implements of understanding, and even what I have taken to be aesthetic lapses, his pose as representative figure, his indulgence of sourness, were in part local texturing of an otherwise abstracted persona, in part doubts frankly cast on the concept of accomplishment, and in part the necessary concomitants of an art so thoroughly engaged. The whole, the work seen as an embodied process of insight and knowledge, forms a synoptic image of the artist's state in a world where men agree only about the variety of intellectual options, where the historical process has rendered men increasingly vulnerable to their own malice, where the multiplicity of knowledge has created greater confusion than understanding, where one after another the comforts of standard solutions have dropped away, where change is the only permanence. In this world the artist is seen not as decorative worker desolated by the loss of patronage and audience but as the responsive man attempting in an indifferent or perhaps hostile universe to assert his integrity and the healing wholeness of his work against the whirling dust of history.

Yeats took great risks, and among them were self-exposure and an ambitious grasp verging on the pretentious. He was not satisfied with the safe, the agreeable. And to a culture that has been so surfeited with easy false solutions that it has eagerly accepted solutions equally unbased because they had the noise of ambition, his poetic practice is a rebuking norm. Turning to it, we might be able better to understand Robert Lowell's *Life Studies,* an attempt to create out of the tradition of the self a more comprehensive image of the person in his variousness. For Lowell's deliberate mussiness in that book originates in an impulse to destroy the carapace of received forms in which his evident genius has been cramped. Like Yeats, he attempts to formulate a state of being in which poetic grace is possible, and he does this by establishing a world of forms in which the poems, multiple in technique and dramatic reference, can have their reverberating life. Lowell does not intend merely to destroy the carapace but to release a more fluent and organic being, closer to the concept of functioning personality moving in a social and religious hierarchy that was Yeats's concern. So too, the long poems of Kenneth Rexroth give resonance to the shorter lyrics, allow the formulation of a world in which the person's fluent identity is more fully visible. And Robert Duncan's work, so carefully and fully wrought, so intensely committed to the rightness of his destiny and experience, also provides an example of a poetry fully aware of its dramatic exigencies and willing to ac-

cept the attendant risks. On a lesser scale, the work of
W. D. Snodgrass, Gary Snyder, and Anne Sexton follow
parallel paths.

The dangers of this motivation are plain. As one re-
viewer recently remarked, the self-revelations of any
son-of-a-bitch might, if such a dramaturgy were followed out thoroughly, become *a priori* acceptable. The
well-made poem would then take secondary place to the
well-made career, the interesting person, and this would
be fatal. What the example of Yeats offers as corrective
is a fuller concept, a clearer recognition of ranges and
troubles that await the modern lyric poet who is attempting to shape an *oeuvre* rather than a set of social
judgments.

And if we move from the central ideas of Yeats's
dramaturgy to his sense of iconography, he displays
also a clear recognition of the stresses placed on the texture of a poet's mind by the disintegration of any symbolic agreement. Moving between symbol and image as
he did, he subjected each significant object that he had
accepted as his responsibility for contemplation to the
rigorous testing of the processes of experience and poetic design. He denied neither tradition nor perception,
and in the multiple examination of thought, object, and
process he remained faithful to the full demands of
experience. His ideas were not in things but in a process of determining relations between external reality,
subjective need, and traditional orders. He achieved,
now playfully, now with fierce intent, a structured order
that is at once free, open, and firmly fixed.

The resulting poetry, phrased in a prosody also tuned
delicately to the maximum accommodation of a complex

world, now takes its place along with that of the greatest writers in English. Its "influence" is impossible to assess, as is the influence of Chaucer, Shakespeare, Donne, Milton, or Wordsworth. It is not so much a store of practice as it is a rebuking norm, to be emulated rather than to be imitated. His poetics, like his poetry, shows us what can be done, it reveals to us possibilities of attainment that keep us from being satisfied with anything less than the very best. Even his failures, in performance or in motive, encourage risk and daring. For, when all is said, Yeats was a very brave poet.

notes

IN THE NOTES THE FOLLOWING ABBREVIATIONS
HAVE BEEN USED:

Auto.: W. B. Yeats, *Autobiography* (New York, 1953).

CP: *The Collected Poems of W. B. Yeats,* definitive edition (New York, 1956).

Essays: W. B. Yeats, *Essays and Introductions* (London, 1961).

Variorum: The Variorum Edition of the Poems of W. B. Yeats, eds. Peter Allt and Russell K. Alspach (New York, 1957).

The above books were published by The Macmillan Company, New York, and by Macmillan & Company, Ltd., London.

Letters: The Letters of W. B. Yeats, ed. Allan Wade (London, 1954).

The *Letters* were published by The Macmillan Company, New York, and by Rupert Hart-Davis, London.

notes to chapter 1
The Embodiment of Truth

[1] Enid Starkie, *Baudelaire* (London, 1957), p. 545.

[2] *Letters*, p. 922.

[3] *Essays*, p. 409.

[4] Starkie, *op. cit.*, p. 541.

[5] *Essays*, p. 346.

[6] Joseph Frank, "The Dehumanization of Art," *The New Republic*, Vol. 140, No. 22 (June 1, 1959), pp. 16–18.

[7] Ortega y Gasset, "The Dehumanization of Art," in *The Dehumanization of Art and Other Essays* (Garden City, N.Y., 1956), p. 11.

[8] Quoted by Charles Edward Gauss, in *The Aesthetic Theories of French Artists, 1855 to the Present* (Baltimore, 1949), p. 57.

[9] *Ibid.*, p. 63.

[10] Guillaume Apollinaire, *Les Peintres Cubistes* (Paris, 1950), pp. 7–8.

[11] Paul Valéry, "Poetry and Abstract Thought," in *The Art of Poetry*, trans. Denise Folliot (New York, 1958), p. 63.

[12] T. S. Eliot, *Selected Essays, 1917–1932* (New York, 1932), p. 7.

[13] F. L. Lucas, *The Decline and Fall of the Romantic Ideal* (New York, 1936), p. 176. Cited by M. H. Abrams in *The Mirror and the Lamp* (New York, 1953), p. 227.

[14] Murry, cited by Abrams, p. 226.

[15] T. S. Eliot, "A Brief Introduction to the Method of Paul Valéry," in Paul Valéry, *Le Serpent*, trans. Mark Wardle (London, 1924), pp. 11–12.

[16] Eliot, *Selected Essays*, pp. 7–8.

[17] Ezra Pound, *Gaudier-Brzeska* (London, 1916), p. 99.

[18] *Ibid.*, p. 98.

[19] *Ibid.*

[20] *Ibid.*, p. 97.

[21] *Essays*, p. viii.

[22] Unpublished MS.

[23] The poems in question are "An Irish Airman Foresees His Death," "Shepherd and Goatherd," "Reprisals," and "In Memory of Major Robert Gregory." For the text of "Reprisals," see *Variorum*, p. 791.

[24] *Letters*, p. 608.

[25] *Letters*, p. 609.

[26] *Letters*, p. 548.

[27] *Ibid.*

[28] Unpublished MS.

[29] *Essays*, p. 509.

[30] *Letters*, p. 675.

[31] *Auto.*, p. 39.

[32] *Auto.*, p. 40.

[33] *Auto.*, p. 53.

[34] *Auto.*, p. 55.

[35] This and the following quotation are from *Auto.*, pp. 62–63.

[36] F. R. Leavis, *New Bearings in English Poetry* (London, 1932), p. 47.

[37] *Auto.*, p. 68.

[38] *Auto.*, pp. 76–77.

[39] *Auto.*, p. 77.

[40] *Ibid.*

[41] *Auto.*, pp. 86–87.

[42] *Auto.*, p. 87.

[43] *Auto.*, p. 88.

[44] *Auto.*, p. 77.

[45] *Auto.*, p. 206.

[46] *Auto.*, p. 93.

[47] "Ego Dominus Tuus," *CP*, p. 159.

[48] *Auto.*, p. 188.

[49] *Essays*, p. 511.

[50] With Lawrence and others Yeats shared a distrust of the abstract that was not merely an aesthetic but a social judgment. See *Auto.*, pp. 116–118.

[51] Yeats was hardly "anti-popular" in his motives, though he was certainly anti-bourgeois.

[52] *Auto.*, p. 118.

[53] *Auto.*, pp. 119–120.

[54] *Auto.*, p. 120.

[55] *Auto.*, p. 125.

[56] *Auto.*, p. 127.

[57] Frank Kermode, *Romantic Image* (London, 1957), p. 19.

[58] *CP*, p. 286.

[59] Plotinus, "Third Ennead," in *The Works of Plotinus*, trans. Stephen MacKenna, vol. 2 (London, 1921), p. 33.

[60] *Ibid.*

[61] *Ibid.*, p. 34.

[62] *Ibid.*

[63] *A Vision* (New York, 1938), p. 86.

[64] Although many of the technical terms of *A Vision* were obviously helpful to Yeats in meditating on his poems, I have not introduced them here because they seem to me to impose unnecessary difficulties in the way of understanding his poetics. What I have done instead is to abstract from *A Vision* concepts rather than nomenclature. The test for me has been immediate relevance to the poetic process.

[65] *Auto.*, p. 62.

[66] *CP*, p. 318.

[67] "The Man and the Echo," *CP*, p. 337.

[68] *Ibid.*, pp. 337–338.

[69] Pardon that for a barren passion's sake,
Although I have come close on forty-nine,
I have no child, I have nothing but a book. . . .
(*CP*, p. 99)

[70] *A Vision* (New York, 1938), p. 83.

[71] *Auto.*, p. 62. (See above, pp. 25–26.)

[72] *CP*, p. 204.

[73] *CP*, p. 205.

[74] *Variorum*, p. 428.

[75] *CP*, p. 264.

[76] See below, pp. 104–106.

[77] Unpublished MS.

[78] Cleanth Brooks, "Yeats: The Poet as Myth-Maker," in *Modern Poetry and the Tradition* (Chapel Hill, N.C., 1939), pp. 173–202.

[79] See Curtis Bradford, "Yeats's Byzantium Poems: A Study of Their Development," *PMLA*, Vol. LXXV (March, 1960), pp. 110–125.

[80] "Cracked Mary," the original name for Crazy Jane, suggests that Yeats had in mind heroic meanings.

[81] For a brilliant study of the persona in nineteenth- and twentieth-century poetry, see George Thaddeus Wright, *The Poet in the Poem* (Berkeley and Los Angeles, Calif., 1960).

[82] See Hugh Kenner, *Gnomon* (New York, 1958), pp. 9–29.

[83] Letter from T. Sturge Moore to W. B. Yeats, April 16, 1930, in *W. B. Yeats and T. Sturge Moore: Their Correspondence, 1901–1937*, ed. Ursula Bridge (New York, 1953), p. 162

[84] *Letters*, p. 742.

[85] *CP*, p. 152.

[86] See Mario Praz, *The Romantic Agony*, trans. Angus Davidson, 2nd edition (London, 1951), esp. pp. 187–271.

[87] See Richard Ellmann, *The Identity of Yeats* (New York, 1954), pp. 172–173.

[88] *CP*, pp. 269–270.

[89] Unpublished MS.

[90] *Essays*, pp. 522–523.

[91] *Essays*, pp. x–xi.

notes to chapter II
Vestiges of Creation

[1] Even the relatively full manuscript of "Among School Children" that Mrs. Yeats provided me with lacks one stage of revisions. In this book, however, I have tried to use relatively complete manuscripts and typescripts.

[2] Cleanth Brooks and Robert

Penn Warren, *Understanding Po-* *etry*, 3rd edition (New York, 1960), p. 164.

[3] The MS reads "And in that faith I live and die." In this context the difference between "and" and the printed "or" seems to me very great. I am not suggesting an emendation to a line that Yeats saw through print several times and therefore (we must assume) accepted. But it is precisely the kind of error that could easily be perpetuated even when not desired.

[4] See below, pp. 104–106.

[5] *Letters*, p. 720.

[6] *Auto.*, p. 122.

[7] *Variorum*, p. 420.

[8] *Letters*, p. 785.

[9] Cf. George Brandon Saul, *Prolegomena to the Study of Yeats's Poems* (Philadelphia, 1957).

[10] Unpublished MS.

[11] A. N. Jeffares, *W. B. Yeats, Man and Poet* (London, 1949). Cf. esp. pp. 159–185.

[12] John Unterecker, *A Reader's Guide to William Butler Yeats* (New York, 1959), pp. 232–233.

[13] Unpublished MS. Succeeding quotations bearing on "After Long Silence" are also from Yeats's MS book. Ellman (*The Identity of Yeats* [New York, 1954], p. 280) quotes the brief notation of "Subject" only.

[14] This is a striking instance of Yeats's evasion of possible mistakes, and it underlines his deliberate and practically unfailing control of tone.

[15] *Variorum*, p. 523.

[16] *Loc. cit.*

[17] Unpublished MS.

[18] Cf. Joseph Hone, *W. B. Yeats, 1865–1939* (New York, 1943), p. 399. The letter to Lady Gregory there adduced is not in *Letters.*

[19] *Letters*, p. 719.

[20] The manuscripts of "Among School Children" henceforth quoted are from unpublished MS material. The poem itself appears in *CP*, pp. 212–214.

[21] "Two Songs from a Play," *CP*, p. 211.

[22] "Nineteen Hundred and Nineteen," *CP*, p. 205.

notes to chapter III

Between Symbol and Image

[1] See the interpretation of these two poems below, pp. 136–146.

[2] F. A. C. Wilson, *W. B. Yeats and Tradition* (London, 1958), p. 23. Although Wilson takes this quotation from Jung's *Psychology and Alchemy,* he accepts the point of view.

[3] Wilson, *op. cit.*, p. 25.

[4] *Ibid.*, p. 236.

[5] *Ibid.*

[6] See Frank Kermode, *Romantic Image* (London, 1957). See also my review in *Sewanee Review*, Vol. 66, No. 4 (Autumn, 1958), pp. 678–685. See also Donald Stauffer, *The Golden Nightingale* (New York, 1949).

[7] *Variorum*, p. 847.

[8] "Baile and Aillinn," *CP*, pp. 396–397.

[9] "Ribh at the Tomb of Baile and Aillinn," *CP*, pp. 282–283.

[10] *CP*, p. 78.

[11] *CP*, pp. 129–130.

[12] Unpublished MS.

[13] W. B. Yeats, "Calvary," in *Collected Plays*, new edition (New York, 1953), pp. 293–294.

[14] W. B. Yeats, *Plays and Controversies* (London, 1923), p. 459.

[15] *Ibid.*

[16] Giorgio Melchiori, *The Whole Mystery of Art* (London, 1960), p. 104.

[17] Unpublished MS.

[18] Plato, "Phaedo," in *Plato's Dialogues*, trans. B. Jowett, 4th edition, Vol. 1 (Oxford, 1953), p. 440.

[19] *CP*, p. 206.

[20] For detailed examination of this poem, see my essay, "The World of Yeats's 'Nineteen Hundred and Nineteen,'" in *The Image of the Work*, English Studies No. 11, University of California Publications (Berkeley

and Los Angeles, Calif., 1955), pp. 211–227.

[21] *CP*, p. 196.

[22] Unpublished MS. The following two quotations are from the same manuscript and have already been quoted by Richard Ellmann in *The Identity of Yeats* (New York, 1954), pp. 176–178.

[23] *Variorum*, p. 441.

[24] *Variorum*, p. 828.

[25] The following two quotations are from a manuscript different from the manuscript considered above. This manuscript is an attempt to rewrite the already printed version of the poem.

[26] *CP*, pp. 211–212.

[27] Unpublished MS.

[28] *CP*, p. 239.

[29] Quoted by Joseph Hone, in *W. B. Yeats, 1865–1939* (New York, 1943), p. 455.

[30] Unpublished MS.

[31] *CP*, p. 240.

[32] Yeats attempted to clear up these shifts in tense when he prepared copy for *The Oxford Book of Modern Verse*. See *Variorum*, p. 490.

[33] Unpublished MS.

[34] *CP*, p. 242. See also *Variorum*, p. 491.

[35] *CP*, p. 213.

[36] *CP*, p. 149.

[37] Letter dated Sept. 6, 1921, in *W. B. Yeats and T. Sturge Moore: Their Correspondence, 1901–1937*, ed. Ursula Bridge (New York, 1953), p. 38.

[38] *CP*, pp. 143–144.
[39] *Auto.*, p. 117.
[40] *Auto.*, p. 223.
[41] *Ibid.*
[42] *Auto.*, pp. 224–225.
[43] *Auto.*, p. 225.
[44] *The Kabbalah Unveiled,* trans., with an introd. by S. L. MacGregor Mathers (New York, 1907), p. 27. I quote from the introduction of the third impression, which, so far as I know, does not differ from the first edition of 1888, with which Yeats was familiar.
[45] *Ibid.*
[46] *Essays*, p. 216.
[47] *Auto.*, p. 14.
[48] Gilbert Murray, *Four Stages of Greek Religion* (New York, 1912), p. 127.
[49] *CP*, p. 80.
[50] "He Wishes His Beloved Were Dead," *CP*, p. 70.
[51] "He Mourns for the Change That Has Come upon Him and His Beloved, and Longs for the End of the World," *CP*, p. 59.
[52] Yeats, *Collected Plays*, p. 245.
[53] *The Works of William Blake,* eds. W. B. Yeats and E. J. Ellis,
Vol. 1 (London, 1893), p. 244.
[54] *CP*, pp. 37–38.
[55] *CP*, pp. 56–57.
[56] *CP*, pp. 57–58.
[57] Yeats, *Collected Plays*, p. 170.
[58] *CP*, pp. 135–136.
[59] *Auto.*, p. 344.
[60] *CP*, pp. 193–194.
[61] "The Tower," *CP*, p. 196.
[62] *CP*, pp. 204–208.
[63] *CP*, pp. 261–262.
[64] *CP*, p. 269.
[65] Unpublished MS.
[66] Unpublished MS.
[67] *CP*, p. 291.
[68] *CP*, p. 211.
[69] *CP*, p. 299.
[70] Quoted in *The Permanence of Yeats*, ed. James Hall and Martin Steinmann (New York, 1950), pp. 338–339.
[71] Unpublished MS.
[72] "The Circus Animals' Desertion," *CP*, p. 336.
[73] Unpublished MS.
[74] *CP*, p. 344.
[75] "The Apparitions," *CP*, p. 332.
[76] "The Man and the Echo," *CP*, p. 338.
[77] *Letters*, p. 922.

notes to chapter iv
The Passionate Syntax

[1] *Essays*, p. 524.
[2] *Letters*, p. 896.
[3] Unpublished MS.
[4] *CP*, p. 257.
[5] Thomas MacDonagh, *Thomas Campion and the Art of English*

Poetry (Dublin, 1913), and *Literature in Ireland: Studies Irish and Anglo-Irish* (New York, 1916).

[6] MacDonagh, *Studies,* p. 79.

[7] *Ibid.,* p. 52.

[8] *Ibid.,* pp. 67–68.

[9] "The Lake Isle of Innisfree," *CP,* p. 39.

[10] "Crazy Jane and Jack the Journeyman," *CP,* p. 253.

[11] Yeats, *Collected Plays,* new edition (New York, 1953), p. 116.

[12] MacDonagh, *Studies,* pp. 72–73.

[13] "The Mother of God," *CP,* p. 244.

[14] "In Memory of Eva Gore-Booth and Con Markiewicz," *CP,* p. 229.

[15] *Ibid.*

[16] "Among School Children," *CP,* p. 213.

[17] *Ibid.*

[18] "Meditations in Time of Civil War," *CP,* p. 201.

[19] Unpublished MS.

[20] Unpublished MS.

[21] *CP,* p. 224.

[22] *Essays,* p. 521.

[23] *Essays,* pp. 521–522.

[24] *Variorum,* pp. 723–724.

[25] This and the following drafts are from the unpublished MSS.

index

inдex

257

DATE DUE

FE 1 3 '68	MY 17 '38		
FE 29 '68	MY 7 '85		
MR 14 '68	AP 5 '88		
FE 19 '69			
MY 21 '69			
DE 3 '69			
MR 9 '71			
AP 1 4 71			
AP 6 '71			
RESERVE			
JE 3 71			
NO 29 71			
DE 16 '71			
FE 3 '72			
AP 20 72			
MY 26 72			
AP 24 73			
MR 10 '81			
GAYLORD			PRINTED IN U.S.A.